MW00491959

"Eric's work has given me the foundation on which I've built my work for the past 25 years as a film and TV director."
—David Anspaugh, director

"What I learned from Eric Morris informs anything worthy I've ever done."
—Hampton Fancher, writer, director

"Since the 1970s Eric has been my colleague, mentor, superb acting teacher and a cherished friend."
—Joan Hotchkis, actor, writer

"If you want to be still and full, Eric teaches the stuff."
—Jack Nicholson, actor

"Eric freed my soul of limitations and taught me how to express my artistic talents. He is one of the greatest teachers of life in the world."
—Scott Steindorff, producer

"Eric Morris has utilized our work masterfully—integrating profound psychological insights into his teachings and providing a unique approach to the craft of acting."
—Hal Stone, Ph.D. & Sidra Stone, Ph.D., clinical psychologists, authors, and creators of Voice Dialogue

"Eric Morris helps actors develop the tools and fundamentals that they take with them throughout their careers. I know. I am one of them. Thanks, Eric."
—Scott Wilson, actor

FREEING

THE ACTOR

An Actor's Desk Reference
with over 140 Exercises and Techniques
to Eliminate Instrumental Obstacles

ALSO BY ERIC MORRIS

No Acting Please (with Joan Hotchkis)
Being & Doing
Irreverent Acting
Acting from the Ultimate Consciousness
Acting, Imaging, and the Unconscious
The Diary of a Professional Experiencer

AUDIO TAPES

The Craft of Acting
The MegApproaches
Imaging for Acting

THE ERIC MORRIS ACTORS WORKSHOP IS LOCATED AT:
5657 Wilshire Blvd. Los Angeles, CA 90036 (323)466-9250

Internet Web site
www.ericmorris.com

FREEING
THE ACTOR

ERIC MORRIS

ERMOR ENTERPRISES

Edited by Carin Galsett

Published by
Ermor Enterprises
8004 Fareholm Drive
Los Angeles, CA 90046

ISBN 978-0-9629709-6-2

This book is dedicated to the memory of

Paul Whitehouse

a wonderful friend, who always supported my writing. He encouraged me to publish my first book, *No Acting Please*, for which he also did the art work. Without him none of my other books would have even been written. I have never known a kinder or better human being. I will continue to miss him.

TABLE OF CONTENTS

INTRODUCTION

This book is for actors, directors and teachers. It is exclusively focused on the actors' instrumental obstacles and problems. Most of the issues that block actors from achieving a relaxed being state will be listed and described in the following pages, as well as the exercises designed to eliminate those problems, which keep actors from being free to act.

Historically, in the training of actors, the instrument has been neglected and overlooked, and, as a result, actors with fewer instrumental blocks have been able to function fairly well, while the others, who may have been even more gifted, were relegated to suffering the obstacles that strangled their talent. From the beginning of my journey as a teacher of acting I struggled against enormous criticism and resistance to the work I was doing to address those obstacles and antidote them. In spite of the hurdles I had to climb over, I was able to create hundreds of instrumental exercises that really work. The results have been life changing for many of the actors who remained on the journey long enough to eliminate their problems and become *free to act*.

Doctors have a *Desk Reference* that they can consult in order to get answers about certain drugs and treatments. In the same way, this book is a desk reference for actors, in which they can find help to address and eliminate the blocks that keep them from functioning. It will also be very helpful to directors who are dealing with actors who have problems in the creative process. I hope that acting teachers who read this book will use many of the exercises herein to help free their students from the blocks and obstacles that keep them from being instrumentally free to act.

THE INSTRUMENT

The instrument is you—your mind, body, voice and emotions. If you were a musician, your instrument would be your violin, harp, piano, saxophone, etc.; but as an actor you have yourself, and that is the instrument you play. The instrument is the vehicle that expresses the talent of the artist, and if it is damaged and cannot function to the optimum of its capabilities, then the artist's talent is seriously inhibited. For example, if the violin a musician is playing is missing a string and the other strings are not taut enough to produce the right sounds, no matter how talented the violinist is, he will be unable to express that talent, as will a pianist who has a piano that is completely out of tune. The same holds true for the actor: Whatever the obstacle is, it will stop him from accessing and expressing his unique talent.

There is no difference between living and acting. Obstacles that plague a person in life become even bigger when he or she tries to act. We grow up in a society with rules and taboos, as well as judgments and criticisms, and when we reach adulthood, we suffer from a multitude of inhibitions, fears, and blocks of all kinds. The unfortunate reality is that most actors pursue their craft and career badly damaged and unable to access the depth of their real talent. In the thirty-two hundred years since the proverbial Thespis stepped out of the Greek chorus and became the first actor, almost nothing has been addressed in the training of actors to liberate their instrument so that they could call upon their talent. Teachers and coaches have sadly neglected the instrumental liberation of the people they train. Lee Strasberg, for whom I have a great deal of respect for the contribution he made to the training of actors, neglected to get deeply involved on a personal level with his actors' instrument. He felt that it would be crossing the line between acting and psychotherapy and refused to even listen to actors describe personal experiences, which he felt were meant for the psychotherapist. So in reality many of the actors with fewer problems functioned better than those with more and greater obstacles. The sad reality is that most likely those with the larger issues were often infinitely more talented than the ones with fewer obstacles.

I have written six other books to date, and many of my exercises and techniques are addressed in those books; so why write another one dealing with issues already discussed and investigated? Well, there are several reasons. One very important one is that I have grown in the many years since I wrote some of those texts; I have improved some of my techniques, which now go further and deeper in certain areas than they did originally, and I have invented new ones. Secondly, unlike the others, this book focuses entirely on the instrument, describing in great detail the problems and obstacles that actors experience. They will be listed in a very specific order, complete with the antidotal exercises to address and eliminate them. In the introduction, I mentioned that this book is much like a *Physicians' Desk Reference*. It lists almost all of the problems that a person can have instrumentally. Under each category there are several techniques and exercises that, in the same way as the entries in a *PDR,* address and alleviate the obstacles. The book can be used to identify whatever stands in the way of the actor's ability to audition, rehearse, and perform. Most of us know how we feel under pressure or when we are obligated and tense about our ability to function successfully. When the issue is addressed, it can be dealt with, and the actor will be free to act.

IMPRESSIVE AND EXPRESSIVE OBSTACLES

Most of the damage to the instrument takes place in the formative and growing-up years. Criticisms, rejections, ridicule, humiliations, and failures cause compensational blocks and behaviors, which create walls of protection from real or imaginary attacks. What occurs? Blocks develop in two instrumental areas: the *impressive* and the *expressive. Impressive* obstacles and blocks are created early and continue as a conditioned response to the onslaught of criticism and other abuses. Walls are erected and shields constructed to block the hurtful stimuli from affecting the person, and consequently, over a period of time, he becomes unaffected by anything that can cause pain or that puts him in emotional jeopardy. In effect, that person throws the baby out with the bath water. When he comes to acting, he has serious obstacles to being affected by most things, and he learns to impose behaviors that do not have an organic source, thereby becoming presentational or representational of what he believes the character is experiencing. Many such actors function on top of what might have been a great well of talent, which will never be accessed because of the *impressive* blocks.

Other people develop *expressive* obstacles. Those actors feel everything but for one reason or another have stopped permitting themselves to express their emotions. It would seem that this would be an easier problem to alleviate. It is not! Over a period of years the inability to express impulses becomes huge, often manifesting as conglomerated emotions that are so entangled with confusion that the person only experiences stress and a kind of emotional morass.

Both of those areas will be addressed in this book. Each instrumental issue will be explored, described, and dealt with in a number of antidotal ways. I have been teaching actors for fifty years and over that period of time have discovered, invented, and explored techniques that work to free the person to act from an experiential place. As I mentioned before, in my early years of teaching I was extremely controversial and accused of doing psychotherapy without a license. I am still considered somewhat controversial, but less so since many of my actors have gone on to great success. As an actor I was aware of my inhibitions, fears, and obstacles, but I didn't know how to free myself from them. In 1959 I started a class with Martin Landau that began to change all that for me. After three years of intense work, which I documented in my last book, *The Diary of a Professional Experiencer,* I had acquired some of the tools I needed. When I began to teach, I explored the problems actors had on stage, and I started working on exercises to liberate those actors from the prison they had been in for the better part of their lives. At one time the number of techniques reached over a thousand, but over the years I have pared them down to a few hundreds.

Almost all of the issues an actor has are related to self-esteem. Most fears and inhibitions stem from a lack of a healthy ego, of self-acceptance and of a sense of entitlement. The work I have been doing for half a century has proven to be life changing, not only for acting, but also for living, because there is no difference between the two.

CONSCIOUSNESS OR THE LACK OF IT

One might wonder why this is mentioned or discussed in a book about the instrument and the obstacles related to it. Well, just about everything we do and everything that inhibits us from being free to do it are related to being conscious. How can we eliminate our obstacles and be free to act if we don't know what they are? Most people have a restricted level of awareness, and their level of consciousness is limited to their survival and personal interests. There are certain training classes, some for law enforcement and others for training employees in various fields of endeavor, where in the middle of the class someone bursts in with a shotgun, waves it around, does some ranting and raving, and runs out of the room. After the incident the group is questioned by the instructor about what the man looked like, the color of his hair and eyes, what he was wearing, what exactly he said and how long the episode lasted, among other questions. In most cases the answers are general and not at all accurate. In order to address and eliminate instrumental obstacles, you have to be aware of their existence and of how to address them.

These are the components of consciousness: observation, awareness, curiosity, commitment and information.

OBSERVATION

Creating a discipline to becoming more observant is like training muscle groups in your body. It is a conscious process that is done with discipline and on a daily basis. Everywhere you go you must deliberately look, observe, question, and train yourself to see and hear everything. Become aware of sounds, odors, essences indigenous to any given environment. Look at something for some minutes, then look away and see if you can actually reconstruct what you observed. Do that every day in various venues, and start training yourself to become observant. Ultimately it becomes a habit that you do not need to tell yourself to do.

AWARENESS

You might think that this is the same as observation, but it is entirely different in its involvement. Becoming aware is a process of paying attention to what is going on in the world, what is happening around you: current events, global warming, gasoline prices, the religious wars, politics, history and its effects on the present, the state of the Union, the world, the universe, and so on. You must train yourself to pay attention, to get out of yourself and get involved.

CURIOSITY

This is probably one of the most important components of consciousness. An actor should find a way to be curious about everything. Children drive their parents crazy asking questions, as in the following dialogue:

"Daddy, why does Mommy cry sometimes?"
"She cries because she is sad."
"Why is she sad?"
"Because something happened that made her feel sad."
"But why did it make her feel sad?"

And so on until Daddy gets impatient and cuts off the child's questions. If this sort of thing is repeated over a long period of time, that child's curiosity finally goes dormant. As an adult, to breathe life back into your childhood curiosity, you must consciously start asking questions of everything, elevate your interest in things that you think don't interest you, and explore the wonderful world we live in with its many miracles.

COMMITMENT

This is a decision you make to do the things you need to do to become conscious. Commit yourself on a daily basis to observe, to elevate and investigate everything that crosses your path, to create a work ethic that allows you to spend time exploring all of the afore-mentioned areas.

INFORMATION

Start becoming informed. Read the newspaper every day, watch the news, read books on many subjects, see movies, listen to the interview programs, seek out and listen to informed people, get into intellectual discussion groups, watch CNN, read magazines on a variety of subjects. Even if fishing doesn't interest you, learn about it. Explore the history of the earth, civilization, religion. Explore the history of the field you're in; create a hunger for information. It is out there.

TENSION

The very first obstacle an actor has to address is tension, because its manifestation acts like a cap on the instrument. It is the actor's archenemy. Historically it has been called by many names: anxiety, nervousness, stage fright, and so on. It is a crippling obstacle for the actor and manifests itself throughout his body. It tightens his muscles; his arms and legs shake or quiver; he gets knots in his stomach and rigidity in his neck and very often feels that he has to urinate, even if he just did. It also affects his voice and pushes all of his impulses down deep into his body, rendering him incapable of being *impressively* affected or *expressively* able to be organic. In effect he learns how to function above the tension and to behave conceptually by denying his real impulses and replacing them with presentational behavior. Over a period of time he can become very successful at denying the tension, compensating for it, and acting above it. Unfortunately, his real talent has been totally suppressed.

Tension has many causes: fear, ego issues, conditioning, track record, prior failures, and so on. There are a great number of exercises that address tension, many of which I have been using in my classes. They work to get rid of the tension on a temporary basis. It is much like using a Band-Aid to cover a very deep wound. Lee Strasberg would spend a great deal of time having actors sit in chairs and do relaxation exercises. He would walk around, lifting the actors' arms and letting them fall to see how much tension the actors were holding on to. Dealing with and eliminating the physical manifestations of tension is a way of freeing oneself temporarily. Unfortunately, the tension returns the very next time an acting obligation appears. It is a chronic affliction, and while it can be dealt with and temporarily eliminated, it will reappear every time there is a responsibility to perform. In *No Acting Please* I described a number of exercises to do away with tension, which I will list again here. In addition, throughout this book I will explore the multifarious causes of tension and attempt to make the actor conscious of how to address them and by so doing eliminate them permanently.

EXERCISES TO ELIMINATE TENSION

LOGY

You do this exercise either in a sitting position or lying down on your back. Start by exaggerating your body weight, becoming heavier and heavier, until it is an effort to move your arms, legs and torso. At that time make an aspirant sound and say, "Logy," repeating the sound and the word throughout the exercise. In addition, imagine that your tension is like liquid and that it leaves your body, creating a pool around you.

I have used Logy for many years at the beginning of each of my classes. In conjunction with Sensitizing and Personal Inventory, it has become part of a preliminary preparation trio that I start my classes with (for more description of this technique refer to *No Acting Please*).

TENSE AND RELAX

To do this exercise you lie on your back either on the floor or on any soft surface. You begin by tensing your muscles at the bottom of your feet and slowly going up your body, maintaining the tension as you go. When you reach the top of your head, you are totally in a rigid, tense position throughout your entire body. You then slowly begin to let go of the tension, moving slowly down your body in small segments, reversing the process. You may repeat this several times if necessary. By doing it you are fatiguing the muscles in your body, which then releases the tension.

RAG DOLL

For this relaxation technique stand straight up and then slowly bend forward towards the floor from the top of your head, one vertebra at a time. Pretend you have a lead weight on the center of your skull that is slowly pulling you down to the floor. When you have bent as far as you can, begin bending your knees, continue slowly towards the ground, and as your rear end touches the floor, slowly crumple to the side and lie down gently. Repeat this exercise if necessary. When you have the room and opportunity to do Rag Doll, it really releases a lot of tension from your body.

DEEP BREATHING

To do this exercise you lie on your back or sit in a chair. Start to breathe, deeply encouraging the air to progressively fill your lungs to their capacity—all the while imaging your body being a hollow vessel, so that each breath you take fills it progressively— going lower and lower until you have filled your entire body with air to the soles of your feet. The process can be repeated until you feel free of physical tension.

WEIGHT AND GRAVITY

Similar to Logy, but without sounds, this exercise is done by exaggerating your weight to the maximum. Each part of your body should be so heavy that it would be very difficult to raise it off the floor. It should take at least ten minutes to fatigue your muscles, thereby releasing the tension.

STRETCH AND YAWN

We all know how satisfying it is to have a good stretch, especially in the morning when waking up. There is nothing more fulfilling than a good yawn, which is also infectious to others. Sitting, standing, or lying on the floor, begin to stretch all of your body to the pleasure point while at the same time yawning with a full, loud sound. Repeat the exercise until the tension in your body is gone.

IMAGING TO RELAXATION

In my fifth book, *Acting, Imaging and the Unconscious,* I specifically detail the process of imaging—what it is and how to do it. By creating various images supported by sense memory, you can achieve a relaxed state and one of pleasure. When you learn the process of imaging, you can add it to your list of techniques for eliminating tension. Imaging, of course, can be used for many other acting responsibilities. It is one of the five MEGAPPROACHES in my system.

OBSERVE, PERCEIVE, AND WONDER

We will be referring to this technique throughout the book. It is used not only to address tension, but also as an incredible selfless-involvement technique. I will describe the process in detail later in the book.

THE TERRIFIC TRIO

This exercise has three parts: *Abandonment, Vesuvius* and *Exorcism.* The actor can do it by himself at home, in any venue that will not disturb the neighbors, or in a class or workshop in front of the group. It is generally used when the actor has so much tension that the other relaxation approaches will not work. When all three parts are completed, the walls of intense tension are cracked, and the actor is free to move on and be ready to work.

Abandonment

The actor usually does this one lying on his back on the floor on a fairly soft surface and having a vocal and physical tantrum, yelling, bellowing, and flailing his arms and legs in the air with total abandonment. This process can continue until he experiences some exhaustion, and then he can stand up and start to do the Vesuvius part.

Once when I was a younger actor, I went on an audition and was so tense that I couldn't remember my own name. I was sitting in the waiting area hoping that they would not call me into the audition room. I was so tense that I knew if I didn't do something right then, not only was I going to blow the audition, but I was sure to humiliate myself, so I went to the restroom, got into one of the stalls, and did a "mini abandonment," making much less noise than in an all out lying-on-the-floor one. I thought that if anyone walked into the toilet they would think that someone was having a difficult bowel movement! It worked: I got the part.

Vesuvius

The actor does this one with a big vocal commitment. Even if he has to start arbitrarily, it has to be loud and very big vocally. It is a large vocal expurgation of all that he is feeling and all the suppressed emotions and tension he has incubated. Even when the exercise is started arbitrarily, it very quickly connects with real emotions.

Example:

"I'm angry. I feel bottled up with rage that I have been afraid to express! I hate the things that I have to do to survive, and I'm sick of people asking me when they can see me in a movie. I'm really pissed at my father. He tries to be supportive, but I hear that *I told you so* in his voice. I'm sick of being scared every time I audition. I feel like my tension is a disease that has no cure. I feel like screaming, yelling. *(He does so.)* My frustration seems to be a bottomless pit. I feel like I'm running as fast as I can but I'm not moving one inch!"

The exercise can go on for as long as the actor is expurgating his impulses or until he is empty of emotions.

Exorcism

With the same amount of large commitment, the actor shouts, "Get out! Get out! Get out!" while at the same time physically pushing forward with both arms, violently thrusting forward with each verbal expression. Instead of being just vocally and physically involved, he should be exorcising real things, people, and situations out of his life. This exercise too can continue until the actor feels liberated.

All three parts of the Terrific Trio should be done one after the other for maximum benefit. In all the years I have been asking actors to do this, I have seen how incredibly effective it has been, especially for actors with very large tension issues. Quite often an actor will jump up on the stage and just do an Abandonment exercise, which frequently is enough to break through that wall of tension.

ALLOW, PERMIT, ACCEPT AND INCLUDE

This technique can be used to address a number of instrumental obstacles; however, when done to eliminate tension, it can be quite effective. The actor can do it alone or in a group, but it seems to work better when she is on the spot. She stands in front of the group and, in a stream-of-consciousness manner, expresses her moment-to-moment impulses and thoughts and follows each expression by saying, "I accept that" or "I permit myself to feel that way" or "I allow that." At first, she may not be convinced of her acceptance, but as she continues the process, she begins to accept and include the things that she is expressing. Everyone doing this exercise should be told that accepting and permitting does not mean approving or liking the issue. It specifically means that this is how the actor feels and that she accepts that she feels that way. She may not like it, but it exists, and she must accept that.

Example:

(Standing erect with her arms comfortable to her sides.) "I'm standing here and I'm self-conscious and uncomfortable. I accept that. I feel impatient, and I allow myself to feel that way. You are all looking at me, and I feel obligated to be interesting, and I accept that I feel that way. I feel like I'm boring everyone. That's OK. I allow myself to feel that. I want to look good. I accept that. I'm still very tense, and I allow myself to be tense. I accept it. I feel like a dork doing this, and I allow myself to feel that way because that is how I feel."

Again this exercise may continue until the actor feels better and more self-accepting, as well as less tense.

One of the problems with tension is that the actor resists the impact of being tense. She refuses to acknowledge it and continues to try to function in spite of it, which only incubates and elevates the tension. By accepting and permitting herself to embrace the many symptoms of tension, she alleviates the strength and impact of it and can release it and feel much more relaxed and ready to work.

MENTAL TENSION

You may be successful in eliminating physical tension, but your brain might be racing with thoughts, fears, obligations and other distractions. There are several exercises that you can do to eliminate mental tension. One of those I have already referred to, and that is *imaging*. There are a great number of images you can create that will allow you to focus on more peaceful things, thereby alleviating the tension in your head. For example, you can create the following image supported by all five senses: You are lying on the sand at a beach in Hawaii. The sun is warm and caressing, and the breeze is filled with the odors of the ocean, suntan oil, and flowers. You feel a sense of well-being, and your thoughts are simple, gentle and without angst or obligation. All of the sensations are created sensorially. This image not only eliminates physical tension but also calms your brain. Another approach to ease mental tension is to focus on an object in your environment and deliberately erase all thoughts, as if you were mesmerized by the object. If you are practiced with meditation, then you may use some of its techniques to clear out mental tension.

All of the exercises above work to eliminate tension in the moment and allow actors to do their craft, but, as I said before, all of them are temporary fixes for a far deeper problem, and the tension will return again and again when an obligation to audition or to act is present once more. All throughout this book there will be approaches to discover the origins of your tensions, as well as various techniques to address them and hopefully eliminate them permanently.

At the source and origin of tension are a variety of problems: a plethora of fears, bad experiences, self-esteem issues, and so on. We are all damaged as we grow up in our society, and not always by mean or evil people. Quite often we are affected negatively by well-meaning parents, teachers, peer groups, friends, religious people, and so on. Things said to us, criticisms or admonishments, can have lifelong effects and erode our confidence and trust in ourselves. If parents, for example, were aware of how one single criticism can affect and damage their child's entire life, maybe they would be more careful in choosing their words.

Tension subsides when an actor becomes secure in a particular circumstance. If he is in an ongoing television series or in a movie where he feels accepted and can function creatively, he achieves a sense of security that eliminates his tension, but as soon as he is out of the situation and obligated to a new project, the tension and obligation return. A number of years ago I was on the telephone with Jack Nicholson, who was preparing to leave for Seattle to do *One Flew over the Cuckoo's Nest.* In our conversation he admitted that he was nervous about that movie. I remember laughing and telling him that he was very much like the character of R.P. McMurphy and that he was, in fact, so close to it that he was not seeing the forest for the trees. I said that in the course of our friendship I had experienced episodes when he behaved in ways that totally paralleled the way McMurphy did, and that I thought he would be great in the role. Of course, he received an Academy Award for that performance. The point here is that even after doing a great number of films and a lot of demanding roles Jack still felt that tension before beginning to work.

Quite often tension manifests itself because we care so much about our work, and if it is not a destructive kind of tension, it can quickly be eliminated by getting involved in the process. I don't know if Jack still experiences tension, but I'm sure that with the amount of success he has achieved, he is probably quite secure with himself and his work. We must not forget that he is a brilliant actor and artist.

FEARS

We all have a multitude of fears. Most of us have learned to live with them. They are, however, blocks and obstacles to the freedom to *be* and *act.* The first step is to recognize them and then to deal with the process of eliminating or silencing them. Being afraid is socially unacceptable, particularly if you are male. It smacks of weakness and is usually hidden from view. When this occurs, the fears are free to cripple us from the inside out. In order to liberate your instrument, you must recognize and acknowledge those fears and deal with them. Again, awareness of a problem is always the first step in eliminating it.

FEAR OF FAILURE

This is a powerful "demon." What the actor usually does is compensate for the fear and redirect his behavior, imposing a false confidence or bravado on top of the fear.

ADDRESSING THE FEAR: THE ANTIDOTAL APPROACH

The first step is to define what is meant by failing. Does it mean not to do a good job? Is it a case of not fulfilling the obligations of the material or the part you are playing? Does it mean that you have limited talent? Is it a way of exposing your lack of craft or process? Is it ignorance? a lack of understanding and an inability to communicate with others? Once you identify the components of your fear, you must acknowledge and embrace it and certainly not hide it from yourself. **You can only fail if you do not learn or grow from the experience.** While it is not advisable to fail in a commercial situation, while doing a film or TV show, you must have an arena in which to explore, experiment, learn and grow; and in that environment **you must allow yourself to fail.** In a class or workshop, while learning a craft, you must embrace failing as part of the evolutionary process. Each time you do an exercise, scene, or monologue, you will experience the results of what you are working for, and quite often you will fail to fulfill the author's intention or the obligation you set for yourself. If you learn something or discover why you failed, then you can reinvest in the process, armed with your discoveries, and can most likely succeed. Failing then becomes a good and necessary thing to achieve craftsmanship. If you can accept and embrace those realities, your fear of failure will evaporate while at the same time you will give yourself the permission to explore and learn, making the whole process an adventure instead of a trauma.

FEAR OF EXPOSURE

The degree to which you protect your sense of privacy will determine the level of your fear of exposure. We all grow up hearing things from our parents about expressing personal and private things: Don't hang your dirty laundry out in public; children should be seen and not heard; if you don't have something nice to say, don't say anything; it's nobody's business. Such instructions and directions influence a child, and he or she grows up being protective of the expression of his or her impulses. That is not a healthy way of life, not to mention that for an actor it is an enormous block to expressive freedom. Organic acting depends on being able to experience what the character is feeling and being able to impulsively express moment-to-moment emotional impulses. An actor who fears exposure will impose emotions that do not come from a real place and will become a conceptual, presentational actor. There are legions of them in our profession.

INTIMATE SHARING AND EXPOSURE

You don't quickly eliminate fears that you have been carrying for the better part of your life. Freeing yourself from conditioning and belief structures is a progressive process. The way to begin might be to relate to a close friend that you trust and to start sharing intimate thoughts and feelings with him or her.

Example:

"You know that we have been friends for a long time, and I have shared many things with you, but I have been reluctant to tell you about my fears and insecurities, partly because I am a very private person and also because I didn't want you to think less of me. I'm afraid of many things: of not being liked, of rejection; I am never myself when talking to a girl; I appear to know what I want to do with my life, but I am totally confused about my goals; I'm often afraid to tell you or anyone when I don't like something you have said or done; I want desperately to act, but I'm terrified that I lack real talent, so I pretend that I'm good."

That is a safe way to start the process of liberation from this specific fear. As you progress with one person, you can expand the intimate sharing to others. You find out that all of your imagined consequences do not appear and that in fact this kind of sharing actually brings you closer to people and elevates relationships to new heights.

If you are in a class where you can do instrumental exercises, you could ask for permission to do some intimate sharing and exposure in front of the class, and with a bigger spot to deal with, the rewards may be even more impressive.

FEAR OF INTIMACY

So many of our fears dovetail into each other. Fear of exposure is part of the protection that keeps us from being emotionally intimate with others. This then becomes a large obstacle to being able to experience intimate feelings and impulses and to express them in a scene. Women seem to have less trouble than men expressing affection and being physical with other people. A lot of scenes in plays and films call for intimate behavior, the expression of affection and love between men and women. In order for it to be real, it must come from a real place. Unfortunately, most of our fears have been with us for a lifetime and are solidly anchored in our persona; so eliminating the various fears that have been conditioned takes repetitious work and tenacity.

There are many causes for the fear of intimacy: fear of judgment, of rejection, of being misunderstood; or growing up in a family that is extremely conservative with affection, tenderness or any outward physical expression of intimate feelings. It is only recently, in the last twenty years or so, that you might see two men hugging each other upon greeting or leaving. Years ago this would have been thought to be highly unacceptable. Society has loosened up to a large degree, and because of television and films and a much looser moral code people have expressed themselves more freely in ways that are now more acceptable than in the past. However, the remnants of the conditioning we grew up with and the fear of exposing our most vulnerable parts keep many of us from being able to be open, soft, warm and intimate.

ANTIDOTAL TECHNIQUES
FOR ELIMINATING THE FEAR

I have always believed that one should not waste any time attempting to break an unwanted habit but more profitably use that time to create a better one.

The first step in addressing and eliminating blocks, obstacles and conditioning is to become conscious of the problem. In this area, for example, once you know you have issues with intimacy, you might ask yourself some important questions:

1. What am I afraid of?

2. What is the worst case scenario, what might happen if I express affection to someone I care about?

3. Will I be judged? thought of as weak?

4. Will I be laughed at or humiliated?

5. What if I get no response and feel as if I had egg on my face?

And so on. Start with an animal—a dog, a cat, or any other pet—yours or someone else's. An animal is not threatening, so expressing affection, petting, kissing, or embracing it will not be intimidating, since most animals love the attention. Next, move on to children—yours, your sister's, brother's, or a friend's. Tell them how much you like or love them, embrace them and allow yourself to feel how that affects you. At first, spend time in those areas, and when you feel a bit more confident, move on to close friends. Start a conversation with, "You know how important our friendship is, right?" and then slowly express your affection. Your friends might not know how to react at first, because it is new for you to behave that way. Expect that, and soon you will be surprised at how openly they will respond to the positive comments. When your courage elevates, you may begin to tell people that you love them. When saying good-bye to people or at the end of a telephone conversation, tell them that you love them. I have many friends I speak to regularly on the phone, and almost always I end our conversation with, "I love you," and almost always they respond in kind by telling me that they love me too. At first, it may be a little awkward, but you will be surprised at how quickly people respond to the expression of love or affection. We all want to be loved, so when we receive affection, we feel validated and accepted. Also encourage yourself to be physical. Give warm handshakes, and hug everyone at appropriate moments, no matter what gender the person is. As you explore and experiment with expressing those things, your confidence will grow, and you will slowly become more intimate with people. It will carry over into your acting, and when you need to be intimately expressive, you will be able to experience those impulses rather than imposing them. If you are in an acting class or workshop, depending on what kind of class it is, you might ask the teacher if you can do specific exercises that elevate your ability to express personal and intimate feelings. For example, ask if you can get up onstage and tell everyone what you feel in the area of intimacy, affection and love. Make one-to-one contact with each person in the class and express personal and intimate feelings: "I really like you. I know that I have never said that before, but I have always wanted to tell you and was afraid to. Jenny, I love your work and would love to do a scene with you. Jack, we haven't really spoken much, but I would like to get to know you, hang out maybe."

Pick out monologues and scenes that are full of intimate emotions, and look for choices from your life that will address the obligations of intimacy.

In my classes when I address a student with fears of intimacy, I have him or her do exercises like the one mentioned above, and I also do *Rock and Stroke,* a two-person exercise that goes like this: usually a woman and the student with the fear sit onstage, and she embraces him and slowly rocks back and forth while stroking his head and shoulders for however long it takes for him to relax into the exercise. The results of this approach are phenomenal. Another one is to have a whole group of people stroke the actor while he is lying face up on the floor of the stage. They all pet and stroke him while at the same time validating him in a variety of areas. This one also has great results.

As is true with any antidotal approach, the exercise must be repeated many times and with inventive variety.

FEAR OF INADEQUACY

This is a very common fear that almost everyone has at one time or another. Objectively one might feel inadequate when one has little or no knowledge or experience in a specific area. If, on the other hand, the actor knows and has been schooled or trained in a specific technique or facility, then it becomes a matter of confidence and trust. Being an actor isn't like being a lawyer or a doctor or part of the corporate world. It is a profession filled with insecurity and unpredictability, so the fear of inadequacy is much greater because of the infrequency of employment. When you do get a job, there is much more riding on your being good.

Self-esteem plays an important part in feeling confident. At the root of almost all instrumental issues is the lack of self-esteem, of a healthy ego, or of entitlement. Later in this book I will spend considerable time addressing this very important issue. Our self-esteem is undercut and damaged in a thousand ways as we grow up in this society, and the damage must be repaired in order for us to have a healthy ego on a permanent basis.

The first step is to identify objectively if you feel inadequate because of a lack of knowledge or training. If you haven't been exposed to the responsibilities or techniques needed for what is expected of you, then you must admit your lack of knowledge and ability in that area and avail yourself of learning what you need to know. Get help, get some coaching or, if necessary, some long-term training. If, on the other hand, you do have the knowledge, training, and ability to address the obligations, then you must do some exercises that will elevate the objective truth, so that you can quell the feeling of being inadequate.

ACKNOWLEDGING YOUR ACCOMPLISHMENTS

This is done audibly or semi-audibly in the form of a sharing monologue. Depending on the area or obligation in question, begin to list what you know about that area and continue to digest the facts about your knowledge and ability to do what is required of you. For example, let us imagine that you feel really insecure about addressing a character obligation in a specific scene. The character is older than you and somewhat physically handicapped by his age and infirmity. You, on the other hand, are younger, stronger and physically athletic. Your fear of inadequacy in addressing this very antithetical obligation is humongous. So in your inventory of accomplishments you list all of your knowledge and facility with the craft that you have so far acquired and experienced.

Example:
"I know how to do sense memory and can create physical liabilities in my body. Having observed older people in the park, I can work for their limitations sensorially. I am also fairly facile with Externals and can work for getting a sense of a specific older person or of an animal that I can translate into human behavior. I also have other techniques that could work to address that character obligation."

The feeling of inadequacy can exist in a variety of areas. The example above is just in that specific area, but the feeling of inadequacy can be an overall self-esteem issue and a recurring theme in your life. See the section on self-esteem for more about that problem.

COUNTING YOUR BLESSINGS

This exercise too is done audibly or semi-audibly in a sharing-monologue framework:

"I am good-looking and healthy; I am intelligent and have done extremely well academically. I am talented; I grasp things quickly; whenever I work, I get great feedback. I know that if I apply myself and concentrate on any problem or obligation, I almost always come up with a positive result; people admire me and are drawn to me; my friends are loyal and supportive; I rarely get criticism that is not helpful," and so on.

IMAGING A POSITIVE OUTCOME

If you are familiar with the imaging techniques, you can create images related to the fears you have about being inadequate to perform and with all five sensory responses see yourself as being outstanding in fulfilling the obligation. You image not only your successful behavior but the responses of all the people involved in the activity. You create great reactions, support and validation of your talent and efforts.

FEAR OF CRITICISM AND JUDGMENT

No one wants to be criticized or judged. The impact of criticism varies with each person, but if the actor has a solid ego and a sense of worth, that impact is less important. It has a huge effect, however, on someone who is doing a scene or working in a film. Most actors avoid the possibility of criticism and judgment by playing it safe, not taking any chances and thereby being predictable and unexciting. A courageous actor will, for instance, experiment, explore choices and attempt to discover the next moment in the next moment. By honoring her impulses she runs the risk of failing to produce the conceptual emotions required in the scene. She is, however, unpredictable and exciting, and if she goes with what her choices stimulate, her behavior might be much more of what the author envisioned. Those kinds of actors are rare. Unfortunately, the fears go back to childhood. We grow up with conditioned, socially acceptable behaviors that we have learned so as to avoid criticism and judgment. There are a number or antidotal exercises and techniques for addressing this fear. Again, the first consideration in dealing with any instrumental problem is to become conscious of it.

ACKNOWLEDGING THE FEAR

Start by asking yourself some questions: Why am I afraid of being criticized? Does it always mean that I am inadequate? Do I accept the criticism on face value without exploring the truth and the source of it? Is criticism always negative? Can I learn something from someone's critical comments, and can those comments help me to grow? Am I perceptive enough to know when the comments are real and when they are projections of the person's own issues? How do I know when a critical comment is valid? When I receive a critical or judgmental comment, what is my first response?

Quite often the first response to a critical comment is to become apologetic or defensive. It is important to acknowledge that response instead of automatically going into a conditioned state.

THE ROUND

I have been doing this exercise for forty or more years. It serves many purposes. I'm listing it in this category of fears because it has great value in recognizing one's fears and being more open to accepting other people's opinions. In the past I would end each class or seminar with a round, so that no one would leave with unexpressed feelings or incubated expressions. The round has four parts: *ego reconstruction, reluctancy, feedback* and *validation*.

The entire group sits in a circle so that everyone can see everyone else. Each person either raises his or her hand to be recognized by the teacher or group leader, or he or she just speaks when there is an opening. All four parts of the round are done simultaneously and can be mixed together. One person can ask for feedback, while the next actor expresses a reluctancy, followed by someone else giving a validation; and the round can continue until it is obvious that there isn't any more to be said.

Ego Reconstruction

This part is an expression by one member of the group to another and is based on observation and perception of the person being related to. The statements are designed to be helpful to that person and his or her growth. All of the "ego reconstructions" should be in the framework of promoting awareness and forward movement. Some statements might be somewhat critical, but the content should always be productive.

Example:

Joe raises his hand to be recognized and says, "You know, Shirley, you are obviously beautiful, and that is a great asset, but I really feel that you might spend more time digging into your feelings and getting down there. I'm not saying that you haven't done some great work in class, but I really feel that you are a much deeper person, and I think that it would be of great value to you and us if you were to excavate that depth." Shirley can only listen to the comment and not respond. The only time there can be a two-way conversation is in the *feedback* part of the round.

Barbara starts to speak after a short silence: "I think that the whole group can do more scene work, and, Harry, you always do good work and you are a hard worker, but you always do the same kind of scene. I think that you should stretch a little and do some other kinds of material. For example, do some comedy. You always do heavy emotional scenes and monologues, and I think maybe you like to cry a lot."

Because the comments are productive and meant to be helpful, the critical element is so much easier to accept. This exercise begins to open the door to relating to criticism in a different way.

Reluctancy

The rule here is to express anything that you are reluctant to say about yourself or to another person. Usually people withhold the things they are reluctant to express. Over a period of time it becomes an inhibition, and many important impulses are pushed down and never see the light of day. Some people incubate their opinions and feelings for their entire life. That isn't healthy for anyone, especially for an actor, who must achieve the ability to be impulsively expressive. This part is done in just the same way as ego reconstruction and validation, with one person speaking at a time.

Example:

Mark indicates that he wants to speak: "I am reluctant to say anything, period, and that's because I don't want anyone to dump any shit on me, so I keep quiet most of the time. I have decided that I must begin to express what I feel, and that's why I am the first one to talk. I am reluctant to say a whole bunch of stuff to a lot of you, so here it goes: Helen, I think you're a snob. I have tried to relate to you on several occasions, and you stiffed me. I don't know who you think you are, but just because I don't make a lot of noise and am not the most popular guy in this class is no reason for you to be rude. Alex, I have reached out to you, called you several times and have not gotten anywhere with you. I think that you too are shy and fearful. *(He looks at the teacher.)* Jack, I think you play favorites in the group. There are certain people you spend more time with, and you let them get away with more stuff. Well, I guess that's all I have the courage to say right now."

There is an uncomfortable silence for a moment or two, and John breaks in: "I think that was fucking great, Mark! You really surprised me."

Joan starts to speak: "I'm reluctant to say that I am happy. I know that might seem a little insipid, but I don't care! I like myself and I like my life, and I don't feel the need to be tragic in order to be respected as an actor."

Alvin raises his hand and gets a nod of permission: "I am feeling discouraged, and I feel like quitting everything: this class, my useless pursuit of an acting career, and this shitty town. I'm sorry to be so negative, but I haven't worked in two years, I only audition occasionally, and I'm sick of waiting on tables. There has to be more to life than this!"

This time there is a longer period of silence, and everyone seems to be somewhat affected by Alvin's reluctancy and somewhat at a loss for a response. Three or four hands go up simultaneously. Ellen is the first to speak: "I have felt exactly that way many times, Alvin, and I identify with you, but you can't throw in the towel. Remember, no one invited any of us to be actors or come to Hollywood to pursue a career. It was our decision to do that. I think you're a talented actor, Alvin, and you just have to hang in there, because one day you might just walk into the right room and, bang, get that part that will do it for you."

Feedback

When I first started to do rounds, there were two kinds of feedback: mind-reading feedback and direct feedback. Mind-reading feedback was done by stating a feeling or conviction that the actor had about what the person he was relating to felt; for example, one actor says to another, "I think you feel that I am a dilettante and don't take this work seriously. Is that what you think?" Over the years I cut the process down to one part, direct feedback, which is the only time in the round when there can be a two-way conversation. It is done in a question-and-answer form. One actor asks someone else in the group for feedback.

Example:

"Chris, what do you think about my work in this class?"

Chris thinks for a moment and responds, "I think that you do good work, but I wish that you would do the work more for yourself. You seem very audience inclusive when you are on the stage, and I wish you would create being somewhere else, work for an environment that not only takes you off the spot but also helps you to create a relationship to the place the character is in."

The first actor then responds to the answer to his question, which is allowed, but the redirect should be brief and not turn into a dialogue: "Why the hell are you so critical of me all the time?"

"It's because I think that you are very talented but extremely lazy and don't work nearly to the level of your ability."

Other people raise their hands and one by one are recognized.

Sally looks at Joe and says, "When I called you last week and asked you to do a scene with me, you said that you were already overbooked with other people in class. Is that true or is it that you don't want to work with me?"

Joe smiles and takes a moment before responding, "No, Sally, I'm not lying to you about being overbooked. I'm doing three scenes now, but I would love to work with you, and if you still want to work together when I'm free, I would love to."

The feedback part of the round allows the students to find out what the real truth is, as opposed to what they imagine. It clears the air and is a very useful tool for dealing with the fear of criticism and judgment.

Validation

This part of the round is probably the most enjoyable and nurturing and as a result of the content elevates the self-esteem of many of the participants. The validation should not in any way be arbitrary but should come from a real place and be a result of perception and having history with, and knowledge of, the person being validated.

Example:

"You know, Peter, I think that you are a really good person. You seem always to be supportive of everyone, and even when you are critical of a person's work, your critique is benevolent and encouraging."

There are no two-way conversations in this part of the round either. Peter can only take in what is said and is not able to respond.

Joan raises her hand and says, "I really like the energy of this whole group. It is supportive and noncompetitive. Alex, you are very easy to be around—no ego trips. I like hanging out with you. Sarah, I know that at times I have hurt your feelings, and I know how sensitive you are, but believe me, I hold you in the highest regard and I know how important you are to this group. *(Several people chime in to agree with that statement.)* I really feel lucky to be here. Jack, you don't say much and you are quiet most of the time, but I think that you are deep, and when you do offer feedback or critique, it is profound. Harold, I love how serious and committed you are to this work."

The validations can continue until everyone has said what he or she wants to express. Not only does validation raise the self-esteem of the people in the group, but it also puts to rest a lot of the incubated and imagined fears.

ACCEPTING CRITIQUE

The word *critique* is important to define. It is a form of criticism, but by the nature of its meaning, it softens the impact of criticism and takes on the character of critical support and encouragement. An actor gets up onstage and faces the audience, and everyone in the group is encouraged to offer a critique to him. It can be related to his personality, prior history, the behavior observed by members of the group; or it can relate to his work in class—his exercises or scene and monologue work. In any case the purpose is to establish a willingness to accept critique, which goes a long way in helping the actor overcome his fear of criticism and judgment.

Example:

(If this exercise is done in a class, the teacher should select an actor who has problems with criticism and judgment.)

John gets up onstage and faces the group. He invites the people in class to give him critique.

Selma raises her hand, is recognized, and speaks to John: "I don't think that you listen well, John. I have noticed that when you are getting feedback after doing a scene you seem to be thinking of your response rather than letting the critique in."

Another hand is raised and recognized: "I agree with Selma. I don't think you care about what we have to say."

A third person chimes in and says, "I think that you are a little arrogant and that you discount what we can contribute to your work."

John can only listen to his critique and not comment verbally. Harry jumps up and begins to speak: "I wish you were more available. I have tried to be your friend for some time now, and you keep me at arm's length. I think you are a great guy, but you are aloof, and I think it's because you are afraid."

Andrea says, "Yeah, John, I wish you would comment more in class. I think you are perceptive and have a lot to say, and I wonder why you don't. Is it because you don't care or you think that your critique might bring retaliation?"

The feedback can continue until everyone who has something to say has said it.

Although this example is for a classroom or workshop, the exercise can also be done on a one-to-one basis. The actor who knows that her fear of criticism and judgment is an obstacle to her impressive and expressive freedom can invite friends to give her critique. If she does that with a number of friends over a period of time, she will become more able to accept and use the input she gets from them, and it will lower her fear of criticism.

BE CRITICAL OF EVERYONE

This is another exercise that I do in my classes. Besides its value in addressing the fear of criticism, it is also a great antidotal exercise for another instrumental obstacle, social obligation, which I will talk about later in the book.

An actor gets up onstage, facing the class, and expresses critical feedback to the various other actors in the group. The rules are: not to be cruel or mean and, if possible, to give productive criticism. However, it is not the same as critique. The reason it is a good exercise to address the fear of criticism and judgment is that the person being critical is taking the chance of being retaliated upon. It also allows the actor to understand the other side of criticism and helps him or her be more open to receiving it.

Example:

"You know—this is for the entire group—I think that when someone gets up here to do something, you should all stop your talking and shit and pay attention. It is rude and selfish of you people to be so self-involved as to get up and go to the john when someone is doing work. And you, Sidney, are one of the worst offenders, reading while I'm doing a monologue. If you want to read, get up and leave the room! For God's sake, Pat, stop, stop chewing your gum so loudly that it distracts everyone in the room! *(She looks at the teacher and addresses him.)* You tolerate too much bullshit from these people, me included. You could demand much more discipline in this class than you do. Joe, your critiques after someone finishes a scene or monologue are totally self-serving and are not meant to help the actor but to demonstrate your incredible insight and knowledge of the work."

Again the exercise can go on for as long as the actor has criticisms to offer the group.

ANTISOCIAL EXPURGATION

This exercise is also done individually onstage in front of the class. It is very large in expression and done in a "Vesuvius" framework. It is loud and expurgatory with physical support. Like many of the exercises and techniques in this book, this one can be used to address a variety of instrumental obstacles: as a release of unexpressed and bottled-up impulses, as an antidote to tension, to eliminate social obligation, or to purge suppressed points of view and antisocial feelings. Used as an antidote for the fear of criticism, it exposes many of the feelings and prejudices incubated by the actor, and it lowers her fear of judgment. Once her points of view are publicly exposed, there is less fear that she will be found out, and then she can personally justify her feelings.

Example:

Starting at the top of her vocal range, the actor says, "I'm sick of being scared about what people think of me. Fuck them all! I'm frustrated with my job. I hate my boss and his petty bullshit. I'm angry about not working enough as an actor, I hate this bullshit business, and I don't give a shit about being right! I hate the traffic in this city. Sometimes I want to jump out of my car and kick the shit out of the guy who just cut me off. You dumb asshole, learn to drive! I'm pissed off at my mother for asking me when she is going to see me on television. *(She can move around on the stage, throw her arms into the air, and generally rant and rave.)* I hate what's going on in this country. I hate the greed that causes banks to fail and companies to go under. I can't even afford to put gas in my car. I'm frustrated and depressed about where my life is going."

This exercise can go on for as long as the expurgations exist. There are, of course, other approaches to dealing with this area of fears. Many of the classroom exercises can also be done on a one-to-one basis or with a small group of friends or other actors.

FEAR OF EMBARRASSMENT

This fear is more common than one would imagine. No one wants to be publicly embarrassed or humiliated, so actors play it safe and do not take chances. They repeat behavior that has worked before and fall into the trap of imposing emotions that do not come from an organic source, thereby short-circuiting their real impulses and making their work presentational and predictable. Over the years I have used a number of exercises and techniques that work to eliminate this fear. When these approaches are used repeatedly over a period of time, they allow the actor to accept the risk of expressing his impulses unpredictably, so he actually discovers the next moment in the next moment and at exactly the same time as the audience. This cluster of exercises is also antidotal for actors who are very self-conscious and are afraid of risking any behavior that makes them feel unsafe.

SILLY DILLY

This exercise is done by an actor onstage in front of the class. He simply makes funny faces, produces strange sounds and encourages his body to find silly and distorted positions. He might speak to people in the class or to imaginary people in a high-pitched and shrill voice. He can sit, stand, lay flat on the floor and make various animal sounds, clucking like a chicken, cawing like a crow or some other kind of bird. If he takes many chances and really courageously stretches his behavior, the rewards will be forthcoming.

GO CRAZY

This exercise is less benign than the previous one. It is a combination of Silly Dilly, Abandonment, and impulsivity rolled into one. It is started with a burst of great energy like an Abandonment exercise, and it is very physical. The silly antics are less predictable and more impulsive and unplanned. The actor uses the entire stage and leaps, twists, turns, making a variety of impulsive sounds and doing silly antics, rolling on the floor and then jumping up like a ballet dancer on drugs. There are no restrictions in movement or sound. He may sing, bellow, screech, and distort his body in very strange positions. The exercise can be physically exhausting, so the actor should stop when he runs out of steam. After doing it a number of times, he will be aware that he not only did not embar-rass himself but also feels freer and realizes that he will almost never be asked to do something as outrageous as that in a play or film.

DISTORTION EXERCISE

Again the actor is alone onstage, facing the class and blatantly distorting her body in various positions, like someone seriously handicapped. She limps around the stage in positions that mirror a contortionist's and at the same time distorts her voice and speech in a similar way. She might speak to the teacher, to the people in class, and possibly do a Shakespearian monologue with the same level of verbal and physical distortion.

AN OUTRAGEOUS MONOLOGUE

Taking a serious monologue from a play or screenplay, the actor says the lines, burlesquing them in various ways and being totally irreverent to the author's intentions. He could take a very serious and moving piece of material and turn it into a slapstick comedy, distorting all of the reality of the piece, or he may do just the opposite, taking a comedic monologue and turning it into a Shakespearian tragedy. His behavior should be exaggerated and theatrical and definitely irreverent. He might take a classical piece and approach it as a street person from Brooklyn. His voice could be distorted in a very high pitch, and he may even change his gen-der behavior.

SLOT MACHINE

This one involves the entire group but is done for the single actor onstage. It is as if she is a slot machine in an arcade. Other actors from the class jump up onto the stage, pretend to put a coin in her mouth, lift her arm up and pull it down, supposedly activating her. Then they proceed to do the most outrageous antics: jumping, falling down, walking like a duck, screaming in various vocal pitches, and so on. The actor who is the machine must imitate all of them, exactly mimicking their every gesture and movement. Each person who gets on the stage to "activate the machine" must do very large and outrageous things. The actor who is the machine doesn't know what to expect, so there is no possibility of her structuring anything or premeditating behavior. The other actors know the purpose of the exercise, so they will design their behaviors to address the needs of the actor onstage. All in all, this exercise is good for everyone. Since the participants are not themselves on the spot, they usually give themselves greater permission to stretch themselves.

PROFESSOR IRWIN KORY

One night, after finishing teaching my class, I was sitting in front of my TV watching Johnny Carson. As usual, I needed an hour or so to unwind after a five- or six-hour class. I had tuned in while the show was in progress. Johnny was talking to this weird, strange-looking man, whose hair stood a foot higher than his forehead. Johnny asked him a question, which I don't remember, and this strange little man launched into a very rapid verbal patter, seemingly answering his question. I listened to what he was saying but kept losing the logic or understanding of what he was talking about. I thought that there was something wrong with me. Maybe I was just fried from the long class, but the harder I tried to follow what he was saying, the more frustrated I became, until I got it: He was a doubletalk artist, and a very good one, because he sounded as though he was making sense, while speaking completely abstract and nonsensical statements. I felt exonerated by my discovery, since I was much too young at the time to be getting Alzheimer's disease!

I immediately saw the possibilities of using this as an exercise in my classes, so I worked with it personally, as I do with every exercise and technique I bring in. I instinctively knew that this would be a very good exercise to address a number of instrumental issues and obstacles, but I had to try out in class first. Over the course of many years I have discovered that this technique works to eliminate a number of obstacles. I use it with actors who have a need to be understood and who go to their intellect instead of their impulses when they act. The exercise antidotes an actor's dependency on logic, as well as on premeditating behavior. It works as a good impulsivity technique, encouraging the actor to irreverently allow himself to be impulsively expressive. In this area of fear of embarrassment it creates a risk level for the actor. His willingness to run the risk of looking foolish or being embarrassed by his behavior or his lack of clarity goes a long way in alleviating his concerns with embarrassment.

Example:

Let us imagine that the interviewer has just been discussing the fact that if a person spent time in space he would not age and that it is gravity that ages us. The double-talker responds, "Yes, that's right, gravity, that does it! A number of years ago I built an anti-gravity machine, and I use it every day. You see I'm really ninety-eight years old, and I don't look a day over forty-five. I eat very light foods, so they don't weigh me down and pull my body closer to the ground—you know, foods with a lot of air in them, such as Cool Whip. I love Cool Whip. I even put it on salads. You see, if you hang upside down from a tree, the blood runs up, not down, the body, and that defies gravity, but not in an oak tree—bad vibes from that kind of tree! You know, it was Sir Isaac Newton who discovered gravity. They say he dropped an apple from a great height, and it fell to the earth, but that's not the truth; it was a wa-termelon, and it hit this lady on the head, and he was arrested and chained to the wall in his cell. It was then that he thought maybe an apple would be better. You know, they have these antigravity weight chambers, and I tried having sex in one of those, but it didn't work. I got it up, but I couldn't get it down! It was also Newton who first had the idea of relativity. He was sitting in that cell, and it came to him that everything was relative. Did it ever occur to you that Australia is totally without gravity? Yes, it is down under, and when they look at the sky, they are looking down, no gravity!"

This exercise can start on any subject and go anywhere. It is done with a lot of energy and conviction and frees the actor from being responsible to be understood and logical. It affords him the freedom and permission to be irreverent, impulsive and whimsical.

Again, all of the exercises listed in this category can be used on a one-to-one basis or in small groups if you are not in a class that works this way.

FEAR OF REJECTION

If this is one of your fears, then maybe you have chosen the wrong profession! Working in any of the arts probably exposes one to more rejection than any other field of endeavor. Actors who have an elevated fear of rejection are usually inhibited, blocked from impulsive expression, and relegated to playing it safe. They create an affable, ingratiating personality that begs for acceptance, and as a result they lose the connection with their true feelings, and reality vanishes. When that happens, being an experiential actor becomes impossible. Many of the exercises already mentioned can be used to address this problem, such as all of the exercises addressing the fear of criticism and judgment and all of the exercises and techniques related to ego and self-esteem, to which I will devote an entire section. However, it is very important to make some mental adjustments in this area, and that requires creating objectivity about rejection.

OBJECTIFYING REJECTION

It is normal to take rejection personally, and it is very difficult not to feel hurt, passed over, insecure about your appearance, abilities, and so on. That is the subjective response, but the rejection may have had absolutely nothing to do with who you are and what you can do. For instance, you have an audition and you do a capable job; you leave, feeling that the reading was pretty good, and you are on a high, until your agent tells you that they went with someone else. You feel disappointed and possibly even depressed about it, when in reality their decision had nothing to do with your audition or how you look. Instead, it was a simple matter of choosing someone who matched up with the other actor playing opposite the character you read for. Quite often it is a decision that is so abstract as to boggle one's mind! Knowing the realities of the business is paramount to dealing with rejection.

INVESTIGATING THE REASONS

After being an actor for many years I acquired the courage to ask a lot of questions when on an audition. I always asked the casting people or the director if there was anything they wanted to tell me beyond what I read in the character description and if there was anything else I should know. I also took the chance of asking them if they felt that I was physically right for the part. You know that you can't lose something that you don't yet have, so why not take that chance? If after reading you feel that you could do it better, ask to read it again. In most cases they will let you do it. Also ask them if they would like you to add anything or make any adjustments to the character or to the emotional content of the material. You would be surprised to learn that most casting people appreciate your commitment to what you are doing. Call your agent and find out what their response was to your audition. You can learn a great deal from what their impression of you and your work was, which goes a long way in allaying your rejection issues.

OBJECTIVE AFFIRMATIONS

On a daily basis you can do some affirmations that will put things in a better perspective:

I am a good person and a good actor, and I deserve to accept that about myself. Not everything that happens to me is a personal response to me or my talent. It is a numbers game, and I have to learn and accept that. If I am trained and ready, then I will succeed more often. My character is not in question, and my value as a person is not in jeopardy. I am who I am, and acting is what I do. I must be able to separate who I am from what I do. I am on a life journey and am fortunate to have discovered my passion.

Learning to accept rejection is a major ingredient to success and happiness.

FEAR OF APPEARING IGNORANT

The concept and the meaning of ignorance have been misinterpreted and misunderstood by people for generations. Ignorance is confused with being stupid or mentally deficient, but none of that is true. Simply stated, ignorance is not knowing something! And if one breaks the word down—IGNOR-ance—then one might understand that the lack of knowing is due to the habit of ignoring knowledge or not being curious enough to expand one's awareness or knowledge in a great variety of areas. Many actors refuse to admit that they don't know the answer to a question put to them, and they will attempt to cover their ignorance in a variety of ways. Let us suppose that you are on a film set, and the director asks you a question about the character's history, based on his background and on the period he lives in. You don't know the answer, so what should you do? Many actors will try to bluff their way through instead of running the risk of appearing ignorant. What you should do is say, "I don't know," and ask for input that you can use in playing the role.

This issue is somewhat more complicated than it might appear to be. The long-range solution to the problem is to elevate your awareness, your curiosity, and your consciousness, as well as to become more informed. I have always believed that an actor is an actor twenty-four hours of every day and that he should find ways to be interested in everything. Read the newspapers, watch the news, listen to people who are informed in their areas, and be curious about what you see, hear, and feel. That is the long-range plan for defeating ignorance and the fear of appearing ignorant; however, there are also short-range antidotes that work in my classes as well as outside of a group.

THE "I DON'T KNOW" EXERCISE

I send one of my students up onstage who I feel has issues in this area, and I ask the class to ask him or her questions about anything: current events, history, acting, and so on, and he or she has to respond with "I don't know," even if he or she does know. The point of the exercise is to let the actor know that it is OK to not know or to say, "I don't know." The sky is not falling!

Example:
"What's your name?"
Response: "I don't know."
"Who is the president of our country?"
"I don't know."
"Where did you grow up?"
"I don't know."
"Why do you want to act?"
"I don't know."
And so on, for however long it takes for the group to run out of questions.

I DON'T KNOW AND ASK TO BE INFORMED

You can do this exercise in the same venue as the previous one or on a one-to-one basis with anyone. When asked a question that you really don't have an answer to, you just say, "I don't know the answer to that, but could you tell me or fill me in on what that is?"

Not only is that an antidote to the fear; it is really very rewarding in terms of what you learn or find out. You will be surprised how people respond to your wanting to be informed. They are flattered or feel that they are doing something good, and the relationship takes on a very interesting quality.

LEARNING HOW TO ASK QUESTIONS

When you know that a specific person has knowledge in a particular area and you would like to know what he or she knows, *ask* that person to talk about it. Be appreciative and learn. It will go a long way in overcoming your fear of being or appearing ignorant. Start with friends and people you feel safe and comfortable with, and then expand into areas that are more intimidating.

FEAR OF BEING VULNERABLE

This is a very common fear and a huge obstacle for actors. Vulnerability is mandatory in order to be affected and emotionally expressive. Being vulnerable, however, connotes being hurt, humiliated, criticized, demeaned, at the mercy of others, and so on. In movies of the forties and fifties and even into the sixties and seventies, you almost never saw a male actor cry in a film. It wasn't considered manly or macho. In later years it became a little more acceptable; however, we grow up in a society that conditions control of emotions and civility. From early childhood we are admonished by our parents: Children should be seen and not heard; boys don't cry; only sissies cry; don't be so emotional! and so on. Most of us have heard those things, not only from our parents, but from siblings, peers, teachers and clergy. Being affectable and expressive is a necessary component of organic acting. If a person is blocked from vulnerability, he cannot truly experience emotional impulses and feelings, so he must impose or assume emotional life that does not come from a real place. Actors who have those obstacles are relegated to being representational actors.

There are many antidotal techniques for addressing this problem. I have used as many as a dozen different exercises to alleviate the conditioned fear of vulnerability.

PRIMAL MOAN

I had been doing this exercise in my classes long before anyone ever heard of Janov and his primal-scream therapy. It is a wonderful approach to breaking through the walls of protection. The actor can also do it alone in his living room. In class he is instructed to get up on the stage, lie on his side in the fetal position with his hands clasped between his thighs, and moan from a very deep place in his body, starting in a low sound and quickly building it into a very large expurgation moan. The sounds have to come from deep in the body and must be held for a long period of time. The exercise should last for six or seven minutes, or longer if the actor can manage it. Quite often I will inject, "Louder, longer sounds, deeper, come from a painful place!" The results are mind-boggling! The exercise opens the actor up to a level of vulnerability and emotional life that is amazing.

COFFIN MONOLOGUE

Another good exercise that works almost every time is this one: the actor imagines that he is sitting in front of the coffin of a dead loved one and is instructed to make that as real as possible. If he is facile with sense memory, he will have more success in creating the coffin and the deceased person. In the framework of an imaginary monologue he talks to the body of the dead person, telling him or her all of the things he feels he never said or would have wished to have said, expressing love, grief and all of the emotions tied into the relationship. The person doesn't really have to be dead. The actor can speak to someone who has not yet passed away or to one who really has. The exercise should continue for however long a period of time is necessary to accomplish a high level of emotional response.

DEATHBED MONOLOGUE

Again onstage, this time lying on his back, the actor is told that he has five minutes left to live, and he is telling the people around his bed all the things that he wants and needs to say before passing on. He can also do this exercise alone in the privacy of his home or in his trailer on a movie set. He talks to all the people in his life he feels it is necessary to make some closure with.

Example:

"I'm sorry, Mom, that I gave you such heartache over my inability to get my life together. I really love you and haven't been able to tell you that. We think that there will be enough time, but it is a mistake to think life is forever. I want to tell you that you have been a wonderful mother, and I don't want you to cry for me. Good-bye, Mom. Gloria, I have always loved you, ever since we were kids, and I'm really sorry for all the abuse and ridicule you took from me. You have been a wonderful sister. Shelley, I'm sorry that I used you. I know how much in love you were with me, and I took advantage of that, and I'm sorry. I wish I could go back and fix everything, but I can't. I really loved you, and I want to say good-bye. George, I know that you have resented me and that we have had a stormy relationship, but I also know we really care about each other, and I will miss every minute of our fights and disagreements. Bye, George. Most of all I'm sorry to be leaving. I feel great remorse for all the things I wanted to say and do, and now it's too late and I'm so sorry."

What usually happens in this exercise is that the actor gets really vulnerable and feels many of the things he is talking about, and when he really begins to believe he is dying, the impact is very compelling.

INTIMATE SHARING

Also in front of a group, the actor begins with a stream of consciousness and moves into a sharing monologue to the people in the group. She emphasizes the meaningful things in her life and is willing to share personal thoughts, feelings, disappointments and frustrations.

Example:

"I'm afraid to do this. I'm afraid to let people see what I'm feeling. I feel isolated a lot of the time. I behave as if everything is just fine, but I don't feel that way. I spend a lot of time alone, and I'm sure that people think I prefer that, but I don't. I'm lonely and find it hard to connect with people. I don't have a romantic relationship and have not had a really close relationship with a man ever, and that's because I'm afraid to reach out and connect with people. A lot of the time I feel alienated from the world. No one knows what's going on inside of me because I never show my deep feelings to anyone. I guess I have been hurt so many times that I have gone into a shell. I want to come out, but I don't know how, and I don't even know how to ask for help. I know a lot of you in this class have been really nice to me, but it doesn't go beyond the time we spend here. I would love to hang out with some of you, and I am attracted to some of the men in this group, but I'm sure that you don't know who you are, because I'm terrified to expose it."

This sharing monologue can go on for as long as the actor wants to share.

I'M JUST A LITTLE BOY/GIRL AND I...

This exercise is done arbitrarily, starting with these sentences: "I'm just a little boy/girl, and nobody loves me. I have no one to play with. I am lonely. I'm lost and I can't find my way home. *(To someone in the group.)* Will you help me get home? *(Waits for a response.)* My mommy and daddy don't love me. They hurt my feelings. I wish I was happy. I'm good, and people don't see that."

The actor can go on, adding as many of the realities as possible. Even though this approach starts out arbitrarily, he gets sucked into it and really becomes quite vulnerable.

There are a great number of other exercises to antidote the fear of being vulnerable:

EXPRESSING DESPERATE WANTS AND NEEDS
I'M DISSATISFIED WITH...UNFULFILLED
EXPRESSING FEARS, LOVE, AND HATE
ANTIPRIVACY EXPOSURE
GET THE DIME
PIQUE AND EXPOSE DEEP NEEDS
HURTS, FEARS, AND INSECURITIES
TRAGIC POCKET

And many more, most of which are detailed in my other books. Most of the techniques listed above that are designed to antidote the fear of being vulnerable also go a long way in the area of overcoming the fear of exposure.

FEAR OF EMOTION

While vulnerability is predominately an "impressive" issue, emotion is both an impressive and an expressive issue. Being affected and being comfortable expressing your responses to the things that affect you constitute the cycle of impressive and expressive freedom. The blatant contradiction among people who want to act is that, though they come to a profession that is dependent on emotional experience, many of them are terrified of experiencing real theatrical emotions. I can't speak with a lot of knowledge or authority about the various countries of our world and their emotional freedom, but I know that Russians, Italians, and Greeks have a reputation for being very emotionally expressive, while in many of the Asian countries, such as China and Japan, people are very inhibited in their emotional expression, and so for the most part are we in the United States. Even though we cannot be compared to the Asian countries, since there is a greater freedom of emotional expression here, there are still some very stifling taboos in certain areas. I grew up in an immigrant Russian Jewish family, and at the dinner table it often sounded like a declaration of war! My brothers and sisters, father and mother were very animated in their expression. Even though I said it sounded like a war zone, there wasn't any anger or conflict. We just had the freedom and permission to express how we felt. That is not the norm in most families, where one must exhibit propriety and control. Some religions also promote a kind of emotional austerity. Because of the suppression of large emotions, many children grow up with that inhibiting conditioning, and they are often drawn to the theater and acting in an unconscious need to liberate what they might feel is there, underneath. It is also true that many of those people just accept their fear and learn to present emotion or imitate what it looks like without ever allowing themselves to truly feel.

The exercises I have created really work, but they must be repeated often over a period of time. They can be used in a classroom, in a workshop setting, in rehearsals, and personally as part of a daily workout schedule. There are no quick-fix miracles. An actor must be dedicated to the total liberation of his instrument, or he will never be able to become an **experiential actor**. The following exercises are just a few that will, if repeated, create trust and confidence that it is OK to be emotional and that the imagined consequences really do not exist.

VESUVIUS

In the section on tension I spoke about the Terrific Trio as an antidote to tension. One of the parts of that trio is Vesuvius. You approach it by decision and arbitrarily by jumping in and very loudly and largely expurgating your frustrations, fears, anger, rage, and anything else that pops up while you are doing the exercise. I have already given an example of how it is done, so refer to that.

ANGER AND RAGE EXPRESSION

This is done much in the same way as you do Vesuvius. The main difference is that you focus exclusively on anger and rage. While in the Vesuvius you may bring in hurts, fears and disappointments, this exercise is a volatile expurgation of red hot anger and rage.

Example:

"I'm angry. *(Repeat that phrase a number of times and then start adding what you are angry about, taking total emotional responsibility for expressing your anger.)* I'm angry. I'm angry. *(Building the size of your anger as you say that phrase.)* I'm angry at the way people treat me. I'm angry at the insensitivity I see all around me. I'm angry at my father for his lack of support. He wants me to be in the corporate world. I feel such anger at his closed-mindedness. I'm angry at how hard it is to pay my bills. I work two jobs and can't make it. I feel such anger that I have so very little time to pursue my acting career. I feel rage at the previous administration. I am so angry at Bush for the thousands of lives lost because of what he did. I feel so helpless that it makes me even angrier. Sometimes I feel that the only way to express my rage is in violent acts," and so on.

The exercise can go on for many minutes and is done at the top of one's vocal range.

CONFLICT ENCOUNTERS

You do this exercise by imaginatively placing an imaginary person in an empty seat and confronting that person in the areas of your conflict with him. If you, the actor, have sensory facility, you might back up the imaginary monologue with sensorially creating the person you are addressing and allowing for that person's responses. The emphasis is conflict, unresolved and angry feelings, and so on.

Example:
"You are a piece of work! You make me sick, always telling me how to live my life, what to do, whom to befriend—and that coming from one of the biggest losers I know. Don't give me that all-knowing, bullshit, smug smile. You are full of shit, and I really don't want you in my life. I don't care that we are related. Blood may be thicker than water, but I'm not getting stuck in its thickness. You are poison to me, and even when I think of you, I get sick. *(Going to another person in the next seat.)* And you, you miserable fuck, stop making promises you never keep. You owe me money, and you never pay it back. You come up with these lame excuses, but I think you are a miserable con artist. Lose my telephone number, you bum! *(To an entire imaginary group.)* Fuck all of you! I don't need your sympathy. If you want to help, prove it!"

The actor can speak to as many people as he or she has conflict with.

ACCUSE AND INDICT

This exercise is somewhat different in emotional content from Conflict Encounters. Even though it has conflict, it also has other emotional colors, such as hurt, pain and remorse. Those colors justify the difference between the two exercises. Again placing an imaginary person in an empty seat, the actor uses an imaginary monologue to confront the person.

Example:
"You were never there for me. You gave me money but never listened to anything I had to say. You were always busy, never had any time to relate. I don't think that you ever loved me. Why did you bring me into this world? You were so busy with your career you hardly noticed me. You didn't even come to my graduation. You were off somewhere pursuing your love life. I think you were closer to your hookers than you were to me. I can't remember a time when you hugged or kissed me. Did you ever? How can you not love your own child? Where does that kind of selfishness come

from? I spent so many years in boarding school that when I would come home for Christmas I felt like I was in a strange place."

The actor can use more than one subject and do the exercise anywhere, in a class or private venue.

SITTING PRIMAL MOAN AND PRIMITIVE SOUNDS

You do this one sitting in a chair, leaning forward in the fetal position with your hands tightly clasped between your thighs. Start to moan from a very deep place just as in the conventional Primal Moan. The rules of the exercise are exactly the same, and the duration is dependent on how emotionally successful you are. At the time when either you or the teacher feels you have reached a level of emotional content, begin to produce primitive animal-like sounds coming from deep in your body. Make sure they are definitely animal, not human, sounds.

ANIMATION AND FREEDOM WORKOUT

Also starting arbitrarily, the actor is instructed to animate every impulse at least a hundred times more than is real, on a moment-to-moment basis. Everything he feels is exaggerated to the max, and at the same time he uses the entire stage area to jump, leap, and include very large physical movements. This exercise is also valuable in other areas of inhibition, such as the fear of being too large or of looking foolish, or just being afraid not to play it safe.

VIRGINIA WOOLF

This is a two-person exercise, and while it is an excellent emotional stretching technique, it is also very good for dealing with the problems of social obligation and conflict phobia. I will describe it in detail when we get to those instrumental obstacles.

THE FEAR OF LOSING CONTROL

Once an actor feels comfortable experiencing and expressing his emotions, he is frequently afraid of losing control and going over the top. If that fear exists, it will often short-circuit him when he is at that place of total emotional involvement. At crucial moments, if the fear appears, the actor will comment about it and totally stop the flow of his organic impulses. The antidote to this problem is experience, which should be acquired in the workshop and in other safe places, such as rehearsals and laboratories. If indeed this is a recognized fear, the actor must find that safe place and push himself with a very impacting stimulus to the very heights of emotionality. If he repeats this many times and discovers that there is no threat of losing control, the problem will evaporate. It is important that he acknowledge the moment of commentary that short-circuits his emotional involvement and at that very moment reinvest in the choice, the impetus that stimulates the emotion. By repetitiously reinvesting he will overcome the glitch.

THE FEAR OF SUCCESS

This is a very complex issue. For years I have heard actors say that they are just as frightened by success as they are by failure. I have been very suspicious of those statements and fears and have often asked actors, "If you were totally guaranteed that you would achieve success and be able to maintain it, would you still fear it?" Usually their answer is, "No, of course not! If I knew for sure that I could handle it and hold on to it, I would not be afraid."

Well then, it seems that the fear is more related to self-esteem and confidence in the ability first to achieve success and then to hold on to it. There are other elements to this issue, which mostly all relate to ego, self-esteem and entitlement: *Do I deserve to be successful? Have I earned the right to succeed? I have always felt as though I ran in the back of the pack. My family always told me not to raise my expectations too high. To this time in my life I have not experienced much success,* and so on. It is very important to discover the origin and the components of this fear and to deal with them directly. I do not feel that the fear of success is a simple fear without cause.

BLOCKS AND OBSTACLES

In this section I will start with emotional blocks. Although there are many crossovers from fears to blocks and obstacles, an emotional block or obstacle can be quite separate from a fear. I have already addressed some of the emotional fears actors have, but an actor can be free of those fears and still have obstacles to expressing certain emotions. I always say in my classes that an actor must be available and accessible to all of the emotional colors of the spectrum. If an actor is comfortable only in certain emotional areas and is blocked from expressing others, that constitutes a limitation of impression and expression. When he is confronted with a stimulus that affects one of those blocks, he will short-circuit the flow of his organic impulses and compensate by imposing the desired emotional response.

CONFLICT

One of the most common inhibitions and blocks is in experiencing and expressing conflict impulses. Almost all drama deals with conflict, and almost every actor will encounter those emotions in his career. If he runs head on into a moment when his behavior must address conflict and he has a block in that area, he will again short-circuit his organic flow by redirecting his expression into another more comfortable area or will impose the emotion from a representational place. A number of exercises address this problem.

ACCUSE AND INDICT

I have already described this exercise earlier in the book, so refer to it.

IMAGINARY MONOLOGUES IN CONFLICT AREAS

Pick people you have been, or presently are, in conflict with. Do an **imaginary monologue** to each of them, emphasizing the areas of conflict between you.

Put each of them in a chair and talk to them as if they were sitting there.

Example:

"You know you have been critical of me for all of my life. You judge me constantly and have always minimized my accomplishments. It has crippled me, and it really hurts, because I love you. I think that your criticism and judgment come from a subjective place. You are an unhappy and unaccomplished person, so you indict me rather than looking to yourself."

Allow imaginatively for the persons' responses to what you are saying to them.

SHARING MONOLOGUES IDENTIFYING THE ORIGIN OF THE CONFLICT OBSTACLE

This can be done out loud or as an inner monologue. You do a sharing monologue in front of a group or by yourself, talking to the world, to God, or to the atmosphere. It is a running monologue about a particular issue or subject. In this case it is done to liberate the components of the obstacle to conflict.

Example:
"As far back as I can remember there were restrictions to our behavior at home. We were never able to raise our voices in anger or criticism. At the dinner table we needed to ask permission to speak, and if there was any element of anger or conflict, we were instructed to bring up the issue in a civilized manner, never allowing our emotions to go beyond what was acceptable behavior. All emotions were stifled except those that were controlled and civilized. My father used to say that strong antisocial emotions were relegated to the lower form of animal life, and that as evolved humans we needed to control our primal emotions. I never heard my father or my mother argue or raise their voices. So I grew up with a conditioned response to conflict, and whenever I felt those emotions, I stuffed them down."

The purpose of doing this exercise is so you can become more aware and conscious of the origin of the block, which will then help you to use techniques to antidote it.

This is a perfect example of a conditioned problem that can be worked on to **repair the damage.** Look further in this book for the section that describes the process used to deal with such issues.

VIRGINIA WOOLF (ONE-PERSON VERSION)

This is a very effective exercise that I have been using in my classes for quite a long time. It is modeled after the play *Who's Afraid of Virginia Woolf,* in which Martha and George spend two hours dismantling each other. They insult, humiliate, and verbally attack each other in this very sick game that they play.

An actor dealing with issues in conflict areas can use a one-person approach for this exercise by talking to several people in his life and being brutally critical and vicious in an imaginary-monologue framework. The difference between this exercise and

Accuse and Indict is that here the purpose is to wound and hurt the other person totally.

Example:

"You are a born loser, do you know that? You have zero talent, and you have accomplished nothing in your life! You're fat and ugly, and you do nothing to change that. It is a waste that you occupy space on this planet, breathing the air and polluting it with your girth. When you die, no one will ever know that you existed or even notice that you are gone. You have contributed nothing to the people in your life and to the earth."

VIRGINIA WOOLF (TWO-PERSON VERSION)

This exercise can be done with another actor or in an acting class essentially in the same way as the previous one, except that the two actors are now relating in a very critical attack mode, trying to outdo each other with the nature of their insults. It is like a one-upmanship involvement, each actor trying to draw the most emotional blood from the other. Both exercises directly address the conflict obstacles and, with repetition, go a long way in eliminating the block.

AGGRESSIVE BEHAVIOR

Being aggressive has always been a social taboo. It is not a behavior that is acceptable in most arenas of life, so people avoid expressing aggressive, hostile impulses. Even when an actor says that when he is acting he can give himself permission to behave in ways he would otherwise never allow, it is very often not true. Whenever a real living obstacle exists, the actor's conditioning will usually stop him from being able to access the behavior from an organic place.

Using the approach technique of **Imaginary Monologues,** select specific people in your life to whom you never expressed what you really felt. Arbitrarily and aggressively confront each of them one at a time with critical and indicting behavior and expressions. Some of the exercises listed above under "Conflict" or those used to deal with social blocks and obstacles can also be helpful in this area.

DEPRESSION AND ANXIETY

Here is yet another obstacle some actors have to confront. In our society depressed people are either shunned or felt sorry for. It is a social condition that brands a person as mentally unhealthy. Since it is not an emotional state that is admired, we avoid showing it in public. That avoidance or redirection becomes a conditioned response to the expression of depression in any social venue.

Almost everyone experiences depression. Depending on its causes, it can last for only a day or two or for a longer period of time. If, however, it becomes chronic, it must be dealt with either in psychotherapy or with prescription drugs. While depression is a universal reality, actors are certainly more prone to it than any other profession. The business is very unpredictable, and an actor can often go months, sometimes years, without employment, which contributes to his being depressed. For him it can become a real obstacle, which he must address in order to be free to act. The first step he must take is to find the cause of his depression by doing a kind of **Personal Inventory** that selectively emphasizes those feelings (see how to do Personal Inventory in the section on emotional insecurities later in the book).

Example:
"I'm depressed. What am I down about? Why am I feeling these dark, hopeless feelings? *(At this point he can expect and wait for a response.)* I'm tired; I haven't worked in a while, and I'm afraid I may never work again! I know that's irrational, but that's the way I feel. I don't feel especially creative right now, and I don't know what to do about that. I have been alone for some time, and I feel very lonely. I don't have a romantic relationship, and that bothers me. I wonder why I have such difficulty with relationships, either getting into one or being able to maintain it."

After doing this exercise, the actor can use a number of techniques to deal with his depression and either eliminate it altogether or soften its impact. Here are a few of them:

THE LITANY OF ACCOMPLISHMENTS

This is done either as an inner sharing monologue or out loud. The actor just begins to list all the things he has accomplished in his life, or he can selectively emphasize his *acting* accomplishments as in the example below.

Example:

"I graduated from a very prestigious university. I started my career while continuing my training as an actor, and I have worked with great coaches. I read the trade papers daily and follow up on casting notices if they fit my type. I have been steadily adding credits to my résumé. While I haven't gotten a running part on a television series, I have gotten callbacks for parts on series episodes. I am in the unions and have been active in them. I am committed to going the distance in this field no matter how long it takes to break through. I am going to take a class as soon as I find the one that is right for me. I'm reading acting books, as well as scene and monologue books for audition material. And even though I get depressed at times, I must stay focused on what I have accomplished."

IMAGING A STATE OF WELL-BEING

Using imaging as a choice approach (see *Acting, Imaging and the Unconscious*), the actor can create being in a variety of relaxed and nourishing environments: lying on the beach in Hawaii, being in a hot tub with someone of the opposite sex, standing on the summit of a very high mountain that he has just climbed, being surrounded by adoring friends, reaching a perfect state of well-being when all is right with him and the world, being dressed in beautiful clothes and filled with spiritual good energy, and so on.

THE DAILY WORK SCHEDULE

A very good way to deal with depression or avoid it totally is to create a daily work schedule that is creative and productive. If the actor is creatively involved most of the time, he will avoid depression. In my book *Being & Doing* I described the process of creating a daily work schedule in a number of areas. The actor can, for instance, spend an hour or more practicing sense memory; he can work on a monologue, exploring the obligations and finding choices that will take him to the fulfillment of those obligations; he can do the monologue, explore the various approaches, work on scenes with other actors, learn the Externals choice approach by going to the zoo and studying animals or by watching people at the Farmers Market or other venues that attract large crowds, read plays, keep up on films, attend seminars and lectures that supply important information about acting, and so on.

PERSPECTIVE INVENTORY

Another important involvement is for you to do a Perspective Inventory frequently, certainly while in the throes of depression but also as part of your workout discipline. It is a simple exercise, which should be done out loud.

Example:
The actor starts with the past: "OK, where was I about two years ago? I was just starting to get involved with acting professionally and was very naïve. Full of piss and vinegar, I hadn't a clue where to start the journey. I was working at a *job-job* and was always tired, and I experienced a lot of frustration at not having enough time to do anything to pursue my career and not knowing how to change things. I spoke to other actors and found that I was not alone in my frustrations, which didn't inspire confidence."

That part of the exercise can go on for as long as the actor has things to list. He can then move into the present: "Now I feel that I have some handles on things. I found a much better job, one that allows me to take off for auditions. My boss understands that I am an actor, and he is supportive. I am in a good acting class and feel that I am learning and growing. I have good friends and a support system. I am working on several scenes at the same time, and I feel very productive. I am receiving good critique from my teacher and the other people in the class. I moved to a better apartment and am actually paying less rent. I feel much more confident in the future. I'm taking better care of my health and going to the gym four times a week," and so on.

He then moves into the future: "Where I want to go is to continue growing as a person and an actor. I want to work more frequently in films and television. I feel less driven than I was in the past, and I want to do many more creative things, such as writing dramatic material, directing scenes in class, and auditioning for professional groups I might join as a member. I want to feel more accomplished as an artist. I want to have an important romantic relationship and eventually start a family."

The actor can go on listing all the things he wants to accomplish and to have in the future.

There are many other ways to deal with, antidote, or avoid depression. I have listed just a few here, but you may find others yourself. Don't become a victim of depression!

SOCIAL OBSTACLES AND BLOCKS

This area is a very common issue for most people and when ingrained over a long period of time becomes a huge obstacle for actors. Most of us are socially obligated to behave in an acceptable way. We are trained and even brainwashed from early childhood on to cut off our impulses if they are not socially acceptable. We have all heard things such as, if you don't have something nice to say, say nothing at all; turn the other cheek; smile, everyone likes it when you smile; do onto others as you would have them do onto you; and so on. Those admonishments have an indelible effect on us as we grow up.

This conditioning has a very stifling effect on an actor. In any play or film there are those scenes where one character socially destroys the other one, and in many cases the behavior is quite brutal. When an actor with rigid social blocks addresses such a circumstance, his conditioning will shut down all connection to the organic realities of hostile aggression, and he will be left with the only alternative: to impose the emotion rather than experience it in reality.

A number of exercises directly address this issue. Hopefully with use and repetition the blocks can be eliminated as obstacles to freedom of expression.

ANTISOCIAL TIRADE

The actor does this exercise by being arbitrarily very big in expression. Almost irrationally and much as in a tantrum, he expurgates all of his antisocial feelings and impulses, many of which he would be terrified to express publicly.

Example:

(Very loud and physically expressive.) "I hate what's happening in the world. The scumbags who run our country are political morons who are sending us down the tubes. We are bankrupt because of the graft and fraud that goes on in the government. The terrorists are taking over the world and should be exterminated. Fuck the police who give tickets to make a quota! They're all a

bunch of moronic imbeciles. I wonder how the 'heroes' would respond if everyone carried a club and a gun. I'm sure they would not be so fucking brave and aggressive, those stupid cocksuckers! I hate the fucking women who wiggle their asses and get offended when you respond to them. Sexual harassment works both ways, and they are just as responsible as men. Fuck women!"

The exercise can go on for as long as the actor has enough antisocial expressions to fuel the rant.

ANTISOCIAL VESUVIUS

This is similar to the antisocial tirade, but what distinguishes it is the nature of the content. While the tirade can be quite exaggerated and manipulated, the Vesuvius comes from a much more real place and consists of things that really irk and upset the actor, stifled opinions that he has been unable to express or expose. This exercise is also done with very big and loud expurgations.

Example:

"I hate the way my mother has been treating me ever since I was a child. I hate her controlling behavior. I am sick and tired of being alone because I have high standards regarding people. I hate having to do shit jobs to support myself. I am an actor and have been in training for years, and I have to wait on tables to pay my rent; and those fucking people who come into the restaurant with their arrogant attitudes and order me around as if I were their own private servant, fuck them! I would like to smash their faces with a plate of pasta. They say that there are more women on the planet than men, so where the fuck are they? I can't get a fucking date! If I drove a BMW, I'd get plenty of dates. Women in Hollywood are looking for men with money or position, so how is that different from being a whore?"

IRRATIONAL TANTRUM

The key word in this approach is *irrational*. The large expurgation doesn't have to make sense. It is more like that of a small child who is having a tantrum and is beating his hands on the floor, screaming and kicking all the while. The actor can start in a standing position or on the floor.

Example:

"No, no, I won't, I won't! You can't make me do it. *(Possibly on your knees beating on the floor and encouraging yourself to be out of control as much physically as verbally and vocally.)* I hate it. No, no, no! *(Screaming.)* You are bad. I don't like you. Get away from here! I hate you. No, no, I won't. You can't make me. They are all bad. No, no, no! *(Screaming.)* Stop it, stop it, stop it! No, I won't do it."

The tantrum can go on for as long as the actor needs to express irrational content.

THE NETWORK *EXERCISE*

I took this exercise from the film *Network* and have been using it successfully for some time. It is quite simple to do. In very large expurgation volume the actor just exclaims, "I'm mad as hell and I'm not going to take it anymore!" He repeats that statement many times, building the volume and emotion with each expression.

THIS IS WHAT I USUALLY SAY, AND THIS IS WHAT I REALLY WANT TO SAY

The actor can do this exercise alone or with another person, but it is much more effective in a group setting, in an acting class filled with people he knows.

Example:

(Standing onstage facing the class.) "I usually say nice things to all of you, because I want to be liked and accepted, but quite often I don't feel like being nice. So I am going to try to express what I really feel; for example, Joe, I always tell you how much I like your work, but I don't tell you that I think that you are lazy and rely on repeating what you have done before. You don't stretch and take any chances, and I don't like the way you relate to me most of the time. You treat me like I am a mascot in this class! I have wanted to say fuck you, Joe, so I am saying it now: Fuck you, Joe! Cindy, I follow you around like a lap dog, because I am so attracted to you; and you know it and use it, and I think that stinks! I want respect from you, and I want you to relate to me as a man, not your gofer. Do you get it? And if you don't, fuck you too! To you the teacher: I am always respectful and complimentary, but I would like you to

spend more time paying attention to me. I'm grateful for what you have taught me, but I don't get real support from you."

In dealing with any block or obstacle, being conscious of the problem is the major step in eliminating it. So much of our life is taken up with responsibilities and preoccupations that we often move through it in a fog. Instead of challenging them, we accept issues and obstacles as a way of life to be dealt with. I have often told my students that I believe that our responsibility in our journey from birth to death is to elevate our consciousness to the highest level possible. If the entire world was dedicated to that developmental journey, there would probably be no wars, prejudice, or hate.

PERSONAL INVENTORY II

Another way to address social blocks and obstacles is to use this exercise on a daily basis. It is done in the same way as Personal Inventory (see the section on emotional insecurities below) except that after responding to the question, *How do I feel?* the actor adds, *Am I expressing how I feel? And if not, why not? And what can I do to express how I feel right now?* In all social circumstances if you are aware of what you are feeling as opposed to how you are behaving, then you can make the adjustment and express your real feelings and impulses.

To use the exercise specifically in this area you must be aware of the social pressure at the time it is occurring. For example, you are having lunch with a friend, and he is being very critical of another one of your friends, and you sit there listening to him bash that other person. Your social block inhibits your ability to say anything contrary to him, but you are feeling angry about the unjust criticism. What you might ordinarily do is nod and say nothing, but if at that very moment you did an inner monologue using Personal Inventory II, it might go like this: *How do I feel about what is being said?* (Acknowledging your real responses in the inner monologue.) *Am I expressing it?* (Again being aware of your real feelings.) *If not, why not?* (Identifying the fear, the block, the social conditioning you grew up with.) *And what can I do about it?*

That entire inner monologue is going on while you are relating to your friend at the table, and at that point you can make the decision to express how you really feel about what is being said: "I think that you are being extremely unfair to the person we both know and like. It is certainly a subjective response, and I encourage you to look into what you are really feeling and why."

It may be difficult at first to go against the grain of conditioning, but the more you do it, the easier it will become, and the feelings of liberation from the obstacle will inspire you to continue to express your real feelings.

SEXUAL OBSTACLES

This is really a Pandora's box and a universal issue. We have all grown up in a Victorian society filled with taboos relating to sex and sexual behavior, with social, religious, or parental pressures, peer group opinions, and gender issues, even though we have come some distance since I was young. In a risky 1943 movie called *The Outlaw,* in one scene, in order to warm him up Jane Russell gets into a bed fully clothed with a man who is wounded. The film created a huge stir, and people even demonstrated against it. So you might say that we have grown up some, but maybe not that much in relation to our conditioning. Certainly, with the advent of the birth-control pill and the subsequent sexual revolution, our sexual habits and freedom loosened up, but AIDS ended the sexual revolution and pushed our sexual freedom back several notches.

For actors, sexual freedom is mandatory, not only because we will confront it in dramatic material and have to be free and open in our expression, but because we need to own our sexuality. What makes people go to the movies to see certain actors? Surely it is because those actors are attractive and in touch with their sexuality. Marilyn Monroe was considered to be a sex goddess, and many other actors are admired for their sexual appeal.

If an actor has obstacles and blocks related to his or her sexuality, much of his or her appeal is cut off. Just imagine being cast in a Tennessee Williams play and having sexual hang-ups. How would you approach characters such as Blanche Dubois and Stanley Kowalski in *A Streetcar Named Desire* or Brick and Maggie in *Cat on a Hot Tin Roof?*—not to mention those in *Suddenly Last Summer* and a host of others.

A lack of sexual freedom and self-acceptance affects the body and the way an actor carries himself and relates to others on the stage. It is an obvious inhibition and distraction from reality.

So what can be done to antidote this block? Well, first it must be recognized by the actor who probably has accepted the obstacle as a normal way of life and is not terribly aware of how it affects his or her behavior. Even when confronting a sexual obligation in a scene, a blocked actor will accommodate his sexual behavior by imposing or presenting a sexual expression. Representational acting is the norm in our business. So many actors function from conceptual origins and end up presenting behavior that has no connection to what they are really feeling in the moment. So I have created a number of exercises over the years that directly address the problem and that, when repeated many times, have been successful in removing the sexual blocks and freeing the actor from lifelong sexual inhibitions. Most of the exercises should be done publicly in a class, with a group of friends, etc. Some can be done privately.

SENSUALIZING

The actor stands up in front of the class and begins to touch himself gently and sensually all over his body, running his hands over his skin, face, arms, legs, thighs and genitals. He is encouraged to make pleasurable sounds while doing this exercise. He might lie down on the floor and continue to feel and affirm himself sensuously. It will probably take him some minutes to overcome his self-consciousness, but when he begins to get involved and enjoy the process, the self-consciousness will dissipate. His fingers should explore his entire body, and he should even touch his face and put his fingers into his mouth.

BLATANT SEXUALITY

This exercise is much more aggressive in nature and requires large sensual and sexual movements, as the actor undulates her pelvic area while touching all of the sexual areas of her body—her breasts and crotch—and making very large movements expressing sexual behavior. She is encouraged to make big sexual sounds and to express sexual desires and needs verbally and even sexual attractions and desires for people watching her. The word *blatant* describes the nature of the exercise. She may relate to objects on the stage—a chair, a pillow, the rug—in a very pornographic way, making love sexually to a chair or whatever object she selects to relate to.

EXPRESSING GRAPHIC SEXUAL DESIRES TO THE PEOPLE WATCHING

Standing up in front of the class the actor selects people he is attracted to and relates to them in a very explicit way.

Example:

"Amanda, I would like to fuck you until your hair caught fire, eat your pussy, and suck on your clit until you couldn't take it anymore. Sarah, I would fuck your brains out. Molly, I would put my cock into every one of your orifices and then come all over your face. I would love to have a group fuck, kissing, sucking, and fucking several of you women at the same time. I could handle all of the women in this class, and we could have a huge circle jerk, each of you taking turns sucking my cock, and the one who gets me to come in her mouth is the winner of the circle jerk."

Yes, it is very raw, and it would take a lot of courage to expose yourself in this manner, but it will go a long way in getting over your sexual inhibitions. I have used all of these exercises with great success.

CREATING SEXUAL FANTASIES, PUBLICLY AND PRIVATELY

Most people have masturbatory fantasies in private and are secure with being able to do that. However, it is a different story when those fantasies are shared publicly, which has the greatest therapeutic value. When a person is masturbating, the fantasies are used to turn her on and eventually bring her to orgasm. The goal is quite different when the fantasies are expressed in front of a group. The element of exposure carries the most value in antidoting sexual blocks. If the actor can be open and expressive in public, it helps her to overcome the fear and inhibitions related to public judgment.

Example:

"I love my body. I like looking at myself totally naked in the mirror. I look at my vagina and love the outline of it. I like putting my fingers into the crack, feeling the wetness between the lips. I imagine a handsome man looking at me at the same time, and I can see his desire for me in his eyes. He approaches me and begins to kiss me on my mouth, moving his tongue inside my mouth. I feel very turned on. He kisses me all over my body, moving slowly down to my pussy, blowing warm air into the opening, teasing me with his tongue. He gently runs his tongue on the inside of each of the lips of my vagina, as I watch everything in the mirror. Watching it like that makes me feel like I am watching someone else doing it, while at the same time I feel the impact of what he is doing to me. I watch him as he disrobes, and I am excited by his muscular body. His cock is huge and beautiful, and I want to feel it inside me, but he hesitates, teasing me as he rubs it against my thigh. Suddenly he lifts me up and carries me to the bed, laying me down gently, kissing me with unrelenting passion. I can't wait anymore, so I plead with him to fuck me."

The fantasy can go on for however long the actor feels involved with it. Doing this in front of a class is extremely liberating and, when repeated, goes a long way towards releasing sexual inhibitions.

RAUNCH AND SLEAZE

This exercise in itself is obnoxious. It is ugly and stretches the boundaries of what seems civilized; but having used it successfully for decades, I must say that it is a great liberator. Also done in front of a group, it is not meant to be pretty or a sexual turn-on, but a courageous exposure for the actor, who is pushing acceptable behavior aside. He expresses ugly, vulgar sexual activities in a tirade of words, talking to the world, a group in a class, or even one person, imaginary or real. It is crude and antisocial.

ASK FOR FEEDBACK (IN SEXUAL AREAS)

Standing in front of a group or class, the actor asks for individual feedback about how he or she is seen sexually by people in the group.

Example:
"I want to know if you think I am attractive. That is a question for the whole group, so if you find me attractive raise your hand. *(Several people respond and she continues.)* Larry, do you think I'm sexy? *(Larry responds positively.)* What do you think is sexy about me, Larry?"

"I think you have a great body, and I love the way you walk. I must say that I have had fantasies about you."

(She smiles and moves on to another person.) "Henry would you like to make love to me? *(Henry turns red, smiles, and nods affirmatively. She continues.)* I want some feedback from the women in the room. How many of you think I'm sexy?" *(Many of the women respond positively and enthusiastically.)*

The actor can take as much time with this exercise as she wants to. Getting objective feedback goes a long way in building sexual confidence. She can ask similar questions of her friends.

I suggest to my students who have blocks in this area to pick scenes and monologues that are very sexual in nature. I recommend the play *Nuts* to my female students. There is an outrageously sexual monologue when Claudia is on the stand in the courtroom. It starts with the line, "I get a hundred for a straight lay."

For the male students I recommend the film *Shampoo*. The male character has an aggressive sexual monologue speaking to his live-in girlfriend.

Antidoting a block or obstacle takes time, since it took the better part of your life to form it, but with commitment and repetition it will disappear.

PHYSICAL BLOCKS

There are quite a number of physical obstacles an actor can have, ranging from being physically unexpressive to reluctance to making physical contact with the other actor. You have all seen actors behave and express emotions where the body seems uninvolved in the expression. It can be related to a physical split, but it isn't always the result of that. (I will get much more specific about splits when I get to that part of the book.) Some actors are unable to include their bodies when embracing or kissing another actor. I call that phenomenon an "A-frame connection." I named it that because it actually looks like an A-frame. The upper part of the actor's body is connected to the other person while the lower part is separated by many inches from the lower part of the other body. Another symptom of physical blocks manifests itself when an actor whose obligation is to be very big in expression does not encourage his body to support the size of the emotional expression.

It is always obvious to an audience when an actor is uncomfortable physically.

Most physical blocks have their origin in childhood, although some blocks are created later in life as the result of criticism or rejection. Over the years I have used a number of exercises in my classes that have been very successful in eliminating the obstacles.

THE POWER PREPARATION

The actor can do this exercise alone, but it has a greater impact for him when he does it in front of a group. He gets up onstage, stands upright, bends forward and down, and then imagines that the power from the earth's core is slowly rising up through the earth, through the floor of the stage, and into his body from the bottom of his feet up through his legs, torso, chest, neck, and head, and bursts out of his mouth with an earsplitting expression of, "Power." As he imagines the power coming through his body, he should actually sensorially and through his muscles feel that energy rising through his entire body. The word "Power" erupts at the top of the energetic flow. Not only does this exercise stimulate physical power, but it also gives the actor a powerful connection with his body.

INGESTATION

A very imaginative exercise, this one too is done in a group setting. The actor stands in front of the group, totally erect to his full height. With a sense of power, his arms held high and outstretched, he begins by imagining that he is ingesting everything in the environment—objects, people, walls, the floor, until there is nothing left but him, who has grown huge, because he is filled with all the people and objects he has ingested. As he ingests, he pulls his arms from high above into his body, imagining that with each gesture of his arms he is taking in someone or something. With each ingestion he produces a very large primal sound, a sound that is like a wild animal's at the height of its primitive state. The actor should feel very big and physically powerful when the exercise is completed, as if he had eaten and ingested everything in the environment.

BODY TALK

This is an exercise that I have been using for quite some time. It directs all expressive energy into the body, so that a person with physical blocks and restrictions begins to depend on his body for expression. The actor stands in front of the class and nonverbally relates to everyone, as a group and individually, only with his body. This is not mime or charades but is like creating another language with and through the body. The actor can use his hands, face, pelvic area, abdomen, feet, or any other part. The goal is for him to communicate feelings and emotions through the movements of his body. At first, it will seem difficult, since we depend so heavily on words, but after a time it will get easier. The trap in this approach is to try to *show* the audience what you want them to understand. The right way to do it is to translate what you feel into physical actions.

ANIMATION AND FREEDOM

This exercise can be used for many purposes. It is an emotional stretching workout for people who need to elevate their emotional expression; however, it is also a good technique for including the body and expanding one's physical expression. The actor standing on the stage begins to exaggerate his impulses and feelings, elevating them a hundred times more than natural. He articulates and enunciates every word, while at the same time, using the entire stage, he jumps, cavorts, dances, and exaggerates all of his movements to equal the size of his verbal expression. His movements can be graceful, like a ballet dancer's, or he can take on the character of a martial artist. He leaps, rolls on the floor, and bellows his words so that they bounce off the walls of the theater. Every movement is large and exaggerated. By doing this he will achieve a sense of physical freedom.

In order to eliminate physical blocks and restrictions the actor must repeat the exercises above many times.

FENCING

This is also a very good technique for eliminating physical obstacles. The actor can take a fencing class or may just mime fencing with an imaginary opponent. He might imitate the swashbuckling movies of Errol Flynn, jumping on stairs and leaping while killing the imaginary enemy.

SHADOWBOXING

This exercise is also a good workout for dealing with physical restrictions.

THE CLASSICAL ACTOR WORKOUT

I have used this exercise for a number of reasons: It is a great exercise for actors who do not speak or articulate clearly or for those who mumble and are inaudible. It can be done using a classical monologue or a contemporary one. The actor begins to speak in the Elizabethan style, using his body in a classical way, exaggerating the style to the max. He should move all over the stage, being flamboyant in all his physical gestures. The exercise can be fun as well as productive. It can almost resemble a characteristic Shakespearean sketch. It is not meant to fulfill the classical style of acting.

PRIMITIVE ABANDONMENT

This is not to be confused with the conventional Abandonment exercise. In this one the actor stands upright and begins to move in rhythmical animal movements, making animal sounds. As she does this, she raises her energy to very high levels. Her voice takes on animal growling sounds, and her movement is very animal-like and abandoned. She can use the entire stage and bounce her arms and legs on the floor, moving more and more like a wild animal. The purpose of this technique is to elicit the primal animal energy and free the body at the same time. For people who are physically restricted this exercise is incredibly liberating.

SUPERMAN/SUPERWOMAN

This is also a very large and energetic workout. The actor stands facing the audience and begins to exclaim that he is Superman. With each expurgation he gets bigger, louder, and physically more active, spreading his arms wide and filling his whole body with power and size.

Example:

"I am Superman. I am Superman. I can leap tall buildings in one bound. I am the man of steel, more powerful than a speeding locomotive, faster than a speeding bullet. I can knock down buildings with one blow. *(At this point the actor might get into expressing what is really super about him.)* I am a superman, smart, attractive, intelligent beyond the norm, talented to the sky. I am a lady-killer. I am super kind, sweet and loving, and I have superhuman senses and sensitivity."

At any point in the exercise the actor can begin to leap as if ready to fly, he can flex his muscles and pretend to lift a heavy object, and so on. If a woman is doing the exercise, she approaches it in a similar way, but the content is somewhat different.

EXTERNALS

This is one of the choice approaches that are actually MEGAPPROACHES. It consists in getting a sense through your body of an animal, a person, an insect, or an inanimate object. To better understand it, refer to the section on Externals in *Irreverent Acting*. This technique can be very physically liberating, depending on the particular choice the actor makes. In other words, if he selects an animal that is very animated, with large aggressive behavior, it will certainly open the doors to physical freedom. To employ this technique, it would be appropriate for the actor to first research it.

INTIMACY BLOCKS

This area of obstacles is very common. We live in a very judgmental society. As children we are often discouraged from making physical contact with others, and there is a great emphasis on privacy. We are cautioned not to let people know too much about us or our families. I have heard many times from my students that they have difficulty letting people close to them. Many married couples complain that their sex is mechanical and lacks intimate connection. This can be an enormous obstacle to the actor, since so many plays and films are about intimate relationships—not to mention that it has an impact on the quality of life.

A perfect example of how children are damaged and inhibited from open expression and intimate feelings is an experience I personally had: My son, Jeff, was in the third or fourth grade at an elementary school in the Valley. He was a happy, expressive kid, who liked communicating with others. One day he brought home a note from his teacher and handed it to me. This is what it said:

> Dear Mr. Morris,
> I am writing this note to you so you can become aware of a problem I am having with your son, Jeffrey. Why does he have to greet verbally and touch all the children when they enter the class? He is very demonstrative, and I find his gregarious behavior disruptive. I would appreciate it if you could curb his outgoing behavior.
> Thank you,
> Miss ———

Needless to say I was shocked and angered by the note. I responded by telling the teacher that we encouraged both our children to be open, free, and sociable and that if that was disruptive and interfered with discipline, I would take my children out of the "concentration camp" they called a school. We did. We sent them to Midtown, a school that welcomed individuality and freedom of expression.

So what can be done to eliminate this problem that has a history of many years of conditioning? I have used a number of exercises to help people open the doors to intimacy. When repeated, they have produced great results in liberating actors from their fears and obstacles in this area.

INTIMATE SHARING AND EXPOSURE

I have already given an example of this exercise in the section on fears, but since it serves a different purpose here, the content is somewhat different. In front of the class or of a group, the actor begins with a stream of consciousness expressing intimately personal feelings. He may acknowledge his fear of exposure, but he continues to share his feelings and impulses with the group.

Example:

"I don't really know where to begin. I'm nervous about doing this, but I know I need to. I am shy, and I know it, and I got that way because my parents were very strict with me and my sister. We were not to have conversations during meals, and we needed to ask to be excused when we were finished with the meal. Neither my mother nor my father ever hugged or kissed me, and I don't remember any physical contact. We had a nanny who was a nazi! She was very German, and we were disciplined in everything we did. We had to go to the toilet at a specific time, even if we didn't need to. I was discouraged from any intimacy with my sister—no hugging, kissing or touching—and I never saw her undressed, even when we were small children. When I started school, it was no different. I went to an exclusive private school, where the discipline was as rigid as it was at home. We sat upright at meals and had to be quiet and still while eating. I was eighteen years old when I graduated from high school, and I had never kissed a girl. My hormones were raging, and I would satisfy myself with masturbation. One time while still in school, I was caught by the schoolmaster and lectured on the evils of self-mutilation. Religion was part of the curriculum in that school, and it was taught by a nun who was what you would see in your worst nightmares. She made sex sound like the greatest sin a person could commit, to be practiced only when you were married and solely for the purpose of procreation and no other reason. When I was in college in a much freer environment, I was unable to communicate on a personal level with almost anyone. There were girls who found me attractive but after a single date refused to see me again. One girl told me that I should take a class in kissing!"

Exercises like that can help expose many of the obstacles that have become conditioned over a lifetime.

INTIMATE SHARING AND EXPOSURE
(TWO-PEOPLE VERSION)

This exercise can be done in a group or just between two people. It is done conversationally, as both people share their most intimate feelings and impulses with each other. The level of exposure would probably be greater because the sharing is limited to just one other person. Both people should be encouraged to take chances and really expose their most meaningful intimate feelings and impulses. They can express how they feel about each other as well as about others. They can be very open and exposing but are never encouraged to violate their privacy. What is private is private and can be kept that way.

ROCK AND STROKE (TWO-PERSON VERSION)

I briefly referred to this exercise in the section on fear of intimacy. It too can be done in a class and has better results if there are people watching. To explain it in more detail: the person with the block is paired with a person of the opposite sex but can also do the exercise with someone of the same gender. They sit down and hug each other. The one without intimacy issues hugs and strokes the other one gently and lovingly, while at the same time whispering affectionate things to him or her. There is complete physical contact, and the stroking should include all of the acceptable parts of the body. The content of the things said should be positive, affirming, and also intimate in nature. The exercise can go on for ten to fifteen minutes or longer if necessary.

ROCK AND STROKE (GROUP VERSION)

In this one the afflicted actor lies down on his back on the stage, while five or six people rock and stroke him, touching parts of his body lovingly and saying very positive and intimate things to him. One of the people can lie down next to him and whisper things into his ear, while the others are feeling, stroking, and affirming him. This can go on for however long it seems productive.

SENTENCE-COMPLETION EXERCISE

This one needs the participation of two people: the actor doing the exercise and someone facilitating him: a coach, teacher, or experienced friend. The facilitator supplies the sentence. In this case the emphasis will be on sentences that address the issue of intimacy. The exercise is not structured to eliminate the block but to make the actor much more aware of it, of what it is and of how and why it is there. The discovery potential is monumental. As a result of what the actor finds out, he can then address the block with greater knowledge and tools.

Here is how it works: The facilitator supplies the beginning of a sentence, which may be, for example, "What scares me about being personal with someone is..." and the actor completes that sentence impulsively. He does not think about how to respond but just says the first thing that comes to his mind. If he is in a class, he makes eye contact with each student one at a time as he says the sentence. He may repeat the same sentence and complete it in a dozen different ways before the facilitator changes it. For example, using the above sentence he could say, "What scares me about being personal with someone is that the person might feel I'm out of line and it is none of my business. *(He moves to the next person and repeats the beginning of the sentence.)* What scares me about being personal with someone is that the person might think that I am rude. *(Moving to the next person and making eye contact.)* What scares me about being personal with someone is my fear that he won't like me."

Possibly at this point the facilitator will change the sentence. The actor repeats and completes it: "My worst fear about being socially physical with anyone is that...she might think I'm coming on to her. *(He moves to the next person repeating the sentence and impulsively filling in the blank.)* My worst fear about being socially physical with anyone is that my parents would not approve of this behavior." Moving on to another person and repeating the sentence, he now completes it with, "they might laugh at me and think I'm immature."

Each of those sentences can be said at least ten times before the facilitator moves on to the next one: "I can't allow anyone to touch me because...I'm afraid that I might like it, and that would be very embarrassing."

Next sentence: "It scares me to be physical with a woman because...I might be sexually attracted to her and she would see that."

The value of this approach is in the element of discovery and awareness that the actor can experience. If he is really impulsive in his responses, very interesting and strange things will come out and can lead him to being able to address his problem from a more evolved place in his life.

RELIGIOUS BLOCKS

This is a very hot-button issue even to write about. The two things people avoid discussing with each other are religion and politics, and there is a good reason for that: People take very seriously their relationship to God and their religious preferences. It is almost impossible—and it can even be blasphemous—to be critical to Christians or Muslims about any part of their beliefs. So many actors who are indoctrinated in a given religion carry with them the guilt and taboos instilled in them by their religious training and conditioning. How this affects them can be described in many ways. It can certainly be very inhibiting to organic and impulsive freedom. I'm afraid that I cannot make any positive suggestions, short of recommending some of the techniques used to antidote brainwashing instituted during the various wars that we as a country have participated in.

SUPERSTITIONS

Many actors will avoid using a choice if they believe that it can be destructive to the person they are creating. For example, when I do Coffin Monologues in my classes and instruct actors to talk to a person they love, many times I have seen them refuse to use a living person as if he or she were dead, believing that they might in some way actually cause that person to die. That is the most egomaniacal belief anyone can entertain! If that were possible, a person could control the entire world just by thinking he could do it.

There are a multitude of superstitions actors hold on to: Don't whistle in your dressing room before a performance; you must carry with you a particular object for good luck; don't tell another actor about an upcoming audition because you or he might jinx it—the list goes on and on and unfortunately people believe in those ridiculous things, which become obstacles to an actor's freedom. There is a joke I often tell in my classes: A priest and his friend go to a boxing match. While they are sitting there, the fighters enter the ring, and one of them kneels down in the corner before the first round and makes the sign of the cross on his head, across his chest, and down to his abdomen. The friend turns to the priest and asks, "Father, do you think that is going to help him?" And the priest responds, "Not if he can't fight."

Here again superstition is the result of conditioning and fear, and the antidote is consciousness and dealing with the elements of reality. If the actor becomes aware of how ridiculous superstition is, he might be able to reprogram his belief structure.

INSECURITIES

Everyone has a variety of insecurities. It is the largest club in the world and has the most members of any club. Insecurities exist in many different areas. If not dealt with, they can become malignant and significantly limit, and in some cases destroy, a person's life. Most people just tolerate them and compensate for the ones they experience, instead of becoming aware and objectifying them. There is a popular concept that you will grow out of many of them in time and that some of the others can be dealt with in therapy. In reality, the longer you maintain an insecurity, the more ingrained it becomes.

OBJECTIFYING AND ALLEVIATING THE INSECURITIES

Objectifying is a process of becoming aware of an insecurity first and then specifically defining it. For example, you might say out loud, "I am insecure about how to behave when I meet people who are very successful and intimidate me." By verbalizing your feeling you expose it openly to your consciousness, and as it is now out in the open, it is not able to subliminally affect you. The next step is to ask yourself, What can I do to eliminate this problem or at least learn how to lower its impact on me? In some cases you have to learn to accept the issue and live with it on a new level of awareness.

PHYSICAL INSECURITIES

There are almost as many insecurities in this area as there are body parts. Actors are even more sensitive than the average person, because their physical instrument is a big part of what they are selling, and they are prone to being infinitely vainer. In the years I have been teaching I have probably heard every physical insecurity known to mankind.

Height: This is a common insecurity, more with male than with female actors. Well, if you are at an age where you know you are not going to grow anymore, there are a number of things you can do to address this one: First, you must acknowledge how you feel about it and somehow accept that this is the height you will achieve for your whole life. Accepting reality allows you to come to terms with the issue and find some peace with it.

There are also some things you can do to maximize your height: Adjust your posture, stand up to your full height, and don't slouch. Wear lifts in your shoes, which will add a couple of inches to your stature. Clothing also has an effect on how tall you look. In the film *In Cold Blood* Robert Blake's costume was structured to make him look dwarfish, since the character he was playing actually had short legs. Blake himself is not very tall, but the outfit really shrank him.

Many actors are—or were—not very tall: Alan Ladd, Edward G. Robinson, Al Pacino, Mickey Rooney, Dustin Hoffman, Tom Cruise, and others. Their careers didn't seem to suffer as a result of their height. If you have a strong ego and self-worth, this insecurity can be put to rest. To help with the objectification, you can do a couple of exercises, personal affirmations about the very thing you feel insecure about.

Example:

I wish I were taller, but I have a great body, and I feel good about the way I look. People don't seem to relate negatively to my height. I deserve to feel good about who I am, and my height isn't who I am.

If you are in a group or a class of any kind, you may just ask for objective feedback about your insecure feelings.

Example:

(Standing in front of the group.) "I feel insecure about my height. It bothers me when I go on an audition or even when I talk to people who are taller than I am, and I would like to get some feedback about the way you people see me."

I really believe that you will get objective and positive responses from people. Try it!

Weight: Legions of people fight weight problems almost for their entire lives. A lot of those who are overweight, underweight, stocky, plump, chunky, and so on, try to hide their weight issues by wearing baggy clothes or dressing in garments that don't cling to their body. This is a problem that can be antidoted. If it really affects you, lose or gain the weight, or if you need help, seek a professional in this area. Besides diet, there is exercise. If you get on a regular program with input from a physical trainer, you will not only lose weight but also shape your body. It will take discipline and resolution to achieve your goal, but it is achievable.

Parts of the Body: Over the years actors have approached me with a plethora of insecurities about all parts of their bodies: their nose, ears, hair, complexion, teeth, mouth, lips, and so on. The conversation usually goes like this:

"Eric," the actor asks, "what do you think about my nose?"

"I would say it's a nose."

"No, I mean do you think it is too big or crooked?"

I always respond the same way: "Do *you* think it's too big or crooked?"

"Yes, I think it is!"

"Well then, why don't you have some plastic surgery done on it if you think it will make you happier and less insecure about it? Or you might just emphasize your talent and get off your nose."

Another question might be:

"Do my ears stick out too far from my head?"

"Do *you* think that your ears stick out too far?"

"Well, yes, I do, but I don't know what to do about it."

"Grow your hair longer on the sides or have your ears surgically pinned back. I know several actors who have had that done. It's simple, and if it will make you less self-conscious, do it!"

Yet another person might say, "I'm losing my hair, and it's killing me. I'm so insecure about the way I look that it affects my auditions and my relationships."

"There are a lot of things you can do: Sometimes a good stylist can make you look as though you had a lot more hair. You can get transplants or a hairpiece. They make them very natural these days. Or you can just accept that your hair is thinning, and you will be able to play many characters who have thinning hair. Hundreds of actors are bald and wear toupees, and many of them are extremely successful in the profession. Lee J. Cobb was totally bald at twenty-four, when he played an older man in the play *Golden Boy.* In his many movie roles he wore a hairpiece."

If you feel that you have a complexion problem, see a dermatologist, get dermabrasion, or select the right skin products to address the problem. If you are not happy with your teeth, get braces, caps, teeth whitener, etc. Almost any physical problem can be solved. If your ego is intact, many of those concerns and insecurities will evaporate. Here again you might try some affirmations and run the problem by some friends, asking for objective responses. Whatever the physical insecurity might be, the first step is to bring it to the surface, objectify it, and find ways to put it to rest. So many insecurities are eliminated by a strong sense of self-worth.

EMOTIONAL INSECURITIES

This is a fairly complex area of insecurities, since it includes both the impressive and expressive areas. So many emotional issues are created in the formative years of our lives, evolve into adulthood, and become ingrained subliminally in our unconscious. So much of our personality is influenced by our family and the environment we grow up in, and if we are impacted by conservative, unexpressive parents and siblings, we learn to protect ourselves from being affected and expressing anything other than what are socially acceptable emotions. If indeed we reach maturity and change our environment, we carry with us the imposed limitations we have been conditioned with. If you choose to be an actor, those limitations are very serious and inhibiting. Here is a list of insecurities that fall into the emotional area:

Being emotionally unavailable
Protecting yourself from being affected by external and internal stimuli
Conditioned lack of awareness about impacting stimuli
Feeling that you don't have a really deep and important emotional fabric
Feeling things but being unable to respond or to express what you feel
Fear of being too emotional
Concern with what other people will think about your emotional expressions
Judgment about what emotions are socially acceptable
Surrounding yourself with emotionally conservative and unexpressive people
Imposing emotional expression without feeling it

Denying the importance of being an emotional person
Rationalizing the importance of being emotional

This area of insecurities is very important for everyone but extremely important if you want to act. To antidote any of the above problems or other issues that are not listed above will take resolution and discipline. I am very adamant about verbalizing emotional insecurities, so that you express them and hear what you are expressing. Repeat the issue many times. Define it, understand it, and begin to change the conditioned state.

ADDRESSING THE IMPRESSIVE INHIBITIONS AND ELEVATING ONE'S VULNERABILITIES IN THOSE AREAS

There are a number of exercises and techniques for becoming more aware and affectable. If you do them repeatedly, ultimately you will resolve the problem and become infinitely more emotionally available.

PERSONAL INVENTORY

In my class each actor who gets up on the stage to do an exercise, scene, or monologue starts with Personal Inventory to find out where he is emotionally in the moment, so that he can start from an identifiable state and from there work to address the emotional responsibilities of the exercise or material. In this case, however, the approach is used to find out what you are feeling and what, if anything, is getting in the way of your experiencing your impulses and feelings.

Example:

"How do I feel? *(The exercise always starts with* how—*asking the question.)* I don't know how I feel. I'm feeling tense, and how do I feel? I'm going blank. How do I feel? I feel a little frustrated. How do I feel? I'm feeling something like a rumbling inside; I don't know what that is. How do I feel? I feel blocked. How do I feel? I'm getting a little angry, and I'm frustrated. How do I feel? I feel disconnected. How do I feel? Like I would like to know how I feel."

This process can go on for as long as the actor wants to do it. He can do it alone or in front of a group of people or other actors in a class. If he does it publicly, there will be an increased state of tension and obligation from being on the spot. For impressively blocked people it will be more difficult to find out what they are feeling, but with repetition more and more feelings will come to the surface.

PERSONAL POINT OF VIEW

Somewhat like Personal Inventory in structure, this exercise is different in that after asking, "How do I feel?" the actor adds the word *about.*

Example:
"How do I feel about this room? It's OK. I don't have any really strong feelings about this place. How do I feel about being watched? I like it and I don't like it. How do I feel about my life? That's a big one. I feel that there is not a single response to that. How do I feel about my life? I'm not fulfilled. What do I mean by that? I feel a lot of dissatisfactions in my relationships with people and romantically, and I feel trapped by my inability to expurgate all this stuff I feel inside. How do I feel about what I just expressed? I feel that I need help and encouragement. How do I feel about being stifled by my parents? I'm angry at them for all the inhibiting rules they laid out for me. How do I feel about the direction I'm going in? Confused, confused. I feel that I would like to break out of my shell and do something outrageous."

Again, this exercise can go on for ten or fifteen minutes, and hopefully the actor will become more aware of what he or she is incubating and feeling.

I AM, I WANT, I NEED, I FEEL

Another in the list of exercises to address the impressive area of emotions, this one too can be done by the actor alone or in a group, and the responses should be impulsive and not premeditated or thought about.

There isn't any order in which it is done. The actor can skip around and express wants, feelings, and needs as they come up impulsively.

Example:

"I want to know what I'm doing. I feel a little foolish. I need to understand this. I'm embarrassed. I feel blank. I don't know what I feel at the moment. *(All responses must be impulsive even if they don't make sense.)* I need...to know how I feel. I want to be good. I need to be successful. I feel crazy doing this. I need to be free. I feel silly. I feel sad. I need to...be happy. I need to be free. I want to know how I feel all the time. I feel exposed. I feel embarrassed. I feel ashamed. I want not to care what people think when I express my feelings. I am tired. I am frustrated. I feel a little better. I want... I don't know what I want. I am here. I am me. I feel OK in this moment. I need to be more aware of who I am. I feel...I don't know how I feel. Shit! I hate not knowing how I feel. I need to impress people. I need to go crazy. I want recognition. I am tired of the struggle. I feel exhausted. I feel anxious all the time. I feel trapped. I need to run away. I am me."

The exercise can go on for as long as the actor feels that he/she can come up with responses. If he/she does this repeatedly, the potential impulsive discoveries can go a long way in helping him/her become more impressively accessible.

PRIMAL MOAN

I have already described this exercise in the section on fears. It is a very good approach for elevating the accessibility of the actor in the impressive area, and it is also great for the expressive area of the actor's instrument.

I'M FIVE YEARS OLD AND I...

This exercise can be practiced alone, even though it works better in front of a group. If you cannot remember back to five, start at a more advanced age, eight years old for example. This should be done in the here and now and not retrospectively.

Example:

"I'm five years old and I...am playing with my toy fire truck... I'm in my bedroom, and there are airplanes on the wallpaper. I'm five years old and I hear my mom in the kitchen...I'm five years old and I...am in kindergarten. I like my teacher...I play with clay and make things out of it. I'm five years old and when I cry, my daddy tells me to stop crying because little boys don't cry. Only girls cry. I'm five years old and I...like the games that I have. *(The actor can stay with five years old until he runs out of things remembered at that age, and then he can move on to six years old.)* I'm six years old and I...am in first grade. I hate my teacher. She is mean and tells me not to talk to the other kids...I like to talk to them...She makes me put my finger in front of my lips to keep quiet. I'm six years old and I like recess, because I can talk to the other kids, mostly the girls...I can yell and scream if I want to. I'm six years old and when we eat dinner, I am told not to talk with my mouth full of food. I'm six years old and I am scared of the dark. I want to sleep with the light on, but my daddy won't let me. I'm six years old and I hate my older sister, because she teases me and makes fun of me. I'm seven years old and I'm in second grade, and I don't like school, but I like my teacher better. I'm seven years old and I want to be eight years old. I'm seven years old and I want to go to the beach. I'm seven years old and I wet the bed, and I'm afraid to tell my mom. I'm seven years old and I like to watch scary movies on the TV, but I can't. They won't let me. I'm eight years old and I like girls a lot. I like Lucille. She sits in the desk in front of me, and I like the way she smells."

This exercise can go all the way into the teen years and beyond. Its value is for you to become aware of the events in your life when the restrictions occurred and thereby address your discoveries by finding techniques to antidote your inhibitions.

SHARING MONOLOGUES

As I explained before, you do a sharing monologue by speaking out loud to the world at large, to a group of people in a class, or when you are alone in your living room. In this case it must be done out loud and not as an inner monologue. You should selectively emphasize things that make you feel vulnerable or that you have some recognizable emotional feelings about, creatively manipulating the sharing monologue to exclusively go into areas that are emotional.

Example:

"I often tear up when watching a movie I am affected by, but I only give myself permission to cry when I am alone in the darkness of a movie theater or when I'm at home by myself watching a movie on television. I am affected when I see children or animals being abused or mistreated. I feel very sad when I think that my parents are getting older and that someday they will be gone. When my relationship with Ellen ended, I was very hurt, sad and depressed, and I wish I could have let her see how I felt. I feel a lot about a lot of things, but sometimes I don't know what those feelings are, and I wish I could bring them up to the surface. My parents always told me that wearing my heart on my sleeve was a sign of weakness and that I should not give others the opportunity to use my feelings against me. When I dream, I often cry, but I'm reluctant to be that emotional at most other times. I even stop myself when I have the impulse to cry."

This exercise is designed to discover and encourage the expression of internalized feelings and helps to address suppressed impulses.

IMAGINARY MONOLOGUES

This choice approach is used in a variety of circumstances, most often to address a choice in a monologue or scene; however, in this instance it is focused on elevating emotions to the surface. Selecting various people in your life whom you know you have an agenda with, feelings for, or an emotional relationship to, you speak to them out loud as if they were there, even though you know that they are not.

Example:

"I know that you love me, but you never say so or express it. I can't remember your hugging me or holding me close to you during all the years of my childhood. Do you know how I feel about that and how that has affected my ability to feel and express love to people I care about? The first woman an infant sees is his mother, and the impact of that on the psyche of a child carries all the way through life, and I know that most of my relationships with women have suffered because I was unable to express my affection, love, and physical warmth to them. *(Moving on to another person.)* Every time I tried to speak to you or touch you in any affectionate or loving way you pushed me away. I know you think it's not masculine for a man to hug his father, but why not? I buried all of my loving feelings deep down, until I couldn't retrieve them. In all the years I have known you, Dad, I have never seen you be outwardly emotional in any area. What kind of life model has that been for me? I'm stifled, scared that if I show any affection or softness people will think I'm gay. I have some gay friends, and I envy their ability to express the way they feel in a multitude of areas, including love and affection. *(Moving on to another person.)* Ellen, I'm sorry it didn't work with us, and I am sure it was because I was so unexpressive of my feelings. Oftentimes I don't even know what I'm feeling, and if an impulse comes up, I quickly push it down. I'm afraid of emotion. I'm threatened by feelings, and I don't know how to change that."

SURROUND YOURSELF WITH MEANINGFUL AND IMPACTING CHOICES

Create, suggest, image people and objects everywhere around you. Everywhere you look there is a person or object that you believe might affect you. Whatever your craft level is, use sense memory and/or imaging if you have the ability to do that, and if you don't, just suggest the objects and people, and imagine that they are there. If you select meaningful people, animals, or parts of memorable places and you relate to them, hopefully you will be affected by them.

Example:
"I'm on the stage, and I look to the left, and I see my dog, Corky. He was there during almost all of my growing-up years, and when he died, I was shattered. I feel some of what I felt, as I continue to relate to him. I'm looking at the back wall behind all the people in the class, and I see my grandfather. He's smiling at me. God, I loved you! You used to hold me on your knee and tell me stories about your life in the old country, and I have never forgotten any one of them all these years. You were the only person I felt it was safe to express myself to. You look warm and soft, and I know that you love me, Grandpa. I look to my right, and I see my childhood friend Anthony. He was my best friend for many years, but he and his family moved to Alaska, and I really miss him. Hi, Anthony, I haven't heard from you for a very long time. I hope you are well. I feel there is someone standing behind me, and for some reason I'm afraid to turn around and see who it is, but I will. Oh, my God, it's Ralph, the bully who made my life a living nightmare all the way through grade school. I hate you, you son of a

bitch! If I ran into you now, I would knock your lights out, you fucking coward!"

The actor might use as many as ten or fifteen different objects to relate to. They must, however, be chosen for their emotional impact.

In an acting class the actor might also get up onstage, sit in a chair, and ask his fellow actors to say words or short phrases that they believe might impressively affect him.

Example:

After the actor gets comfortable facing the class, his fellow students volunteer one at a time to suggest things to him.

Sarah raises her hand and starts the exercise: "You know, John, that I have always liked you."

Joe chimes in with, "I think that you are a very special guy."

Someone else says, "Corky."

Another actor asks him if he has ever lost anyone. Allan says, "I think you are very deep and have a lot to offer."

All the feedback is designed to have an impact on him emotionally. He must just sit there and say nothing, letting everything in.

ALLOW, PERMIT, ACCEPT AND INCLUDE

I have already described this exercise in the section on tension earlier in the book, but as I said then, this approach can be used to address a number of instrumental obstacles. In this instance the emphasis is on feelings and impulses that originate from an emotional place. The actor can do it when she is alone, but it would most likely have better results in front of a group.

Example:

The actor gets up onstage in front of the group and starts the exercise: "I'm reluctant to say anything. I accept that I'm feeling a lot of things, and I'm not sure what they are, and I allow myself to feel that way. I'm afraid of what might pop out of my mouth, and I permit myself to feel that way. I feel that you are bored with me, and I accept that it makes me feel less than, and I permit myself to feel that way. I desperately want all of you to like and respect me, and while that makes me feel a little like I'm on the suck, I accept that I said it, and I accept that I feel that way. I feel rumbly, and I don't know exactly what those feelings are, and it's OK, and I accept it. I often feel things, and I'm not sure what they are, but I know that I feel them, and I allow myself to feel that way. I have a lot of anger and resentment towards my parents for crippling me emotionally, and I accept that."

As she does this, hopefully a lot more of what goes on internally will come to the surface.

ADDRESSING THE EXPRESSIVE INHIBITIONS AND INSECURITIES

As I said earlier, blocks and insecurities exist in both impressive and expressive areas. Some people feel a great deal but are unable to express what they feel, and this phenomenon can be the result of many influences. I have mentioned in this book and in some of my other books that the impact of a single statement or admonishment from an important person can damage a person for a lifetime unless the damage is repaired. Your father tells you to stop being so loud, to stop crying. He says, "You are too emotional. Get a hold of yourself! Don't be a baby! Be strong, not like a simpering girl," and so on. Over a period of time those kinds of criticisms can totally inhibit a person from being emotionally expressive. There are many exercises that I have used in my teaching to antidote those blocks and liberate actors to be emotionally expressive. All of the exercises that I used in the section on the fear of emotion can be applied to this area. Here are a few more:

PASSIONS WORKOUT

This exercise too is liberating and uplifting at the same time. Again, the actor may do this alone or in a group. It is done in a standing position and is approached with great animation. Even if that animation is arbitrary at the beginning, it will soon connect to the actor's real feelings.

Example:

Starting with a lot of expressive energy and animation, the actor says, "I'm passionate about being alive. I'm passionate about where I live. It's beautiful. I love nature. I'm passionate about the ocean. I feel passion about the people in my life. I love them. I'm passionate about being an actor and having made that choice for my life. I feel passion for homeless people. I wish I could help all of them. I'm passionate about exercise and working out. I'm addicted to it, and I really love the feeling after a great workout. I'm passionate about making love. I love kissing my girlfriend. I'm passionate about her, the way she looks, smells, and feels. I'm passionate about having a good night sleep and waking up feeling good. I'm passionate about being healthy. I feel passion about expressing big emotions and purging my feelings."

Here again there isn't any time limit on how long the exercise should go on for, probably until the actor runs out of passions.

LITANY OF WOES

This is usually done by an actor who has difficulty getting into depressive or woeful emotional areas of expression. It is, however, a good exercise for liberating a person's emotional expression. It is structured as a sharing monologue that emphasizes the depressive emotional areas. You can do it in a standing or sitting position, alone or in a group.

Example:

"I'm always in a war about having enough money to pay my bills. It keeps me up at night, and my anxiety level has gone through the roof. I haven't had an acting gig in six months, and it makes me wonder why I still hang on to acting. I'm sick of being a waitress and taking shit from people. I need the job, but they treat me badly. I feel humiliated when my brother or anyone in my family asks me when I'm going to be in a movie. I haven't been in a happy relationship in so long I can't remember when I was. I hate my apartment. It's so grungy, and it smells old and mildewed. I need to buy some new clothes, but I don't have the money, and I don't know when I will have it. I get really depressed thinking that my entire life could be the way it is now. I've been thinking of what it might be like to be in some kind of coma, wake up, and everything would be different. I was once involved with a man who lived in his depressive state twenty-four/seven. He would look out the window and say, 'My life sucks.' I couldn't imagine feeling that way at the time, but now I think that *my* life sucks."

The exercise is successful if the actor achieves a woeful and depressive state.

EXPRESSING FEARS, LOVE, AND HATE

The actor does this one in a large commitment way, in the same way as a Vesuvius exercise, emphasizing all of his fears, everything and everyone he loves, as well as everything he hates.

Example:

"I'm afraid of dying. I'm afraid that I won't make it and that I will be the loser that my father thinks I am. I hate the way he thinks and his bullshit morality. I hate organized religion and all the tragedy that it has brought on the world. I love my friends, and I love to be able to kick back and veg out. I love my girlfriend and the way she treats me. I'm afraid that I might lose her if I don't make a bigger commitment to the relationship. I fear getting sick and not being able to take care of myself. I love watching movies. I hate that I'm not in them. I'm afraid of the unknown and the supernatural. I love when I'm acting and it feels right. I love when I'm not afraid to express what I feel, even when it isn't popular. I hate lying politicians and the bullshit they try to ram down our throats. I love this country. I love what it is founded on, but I hate the people who distort democracy."

This exercise is very liberating emotionally and can go on for as long as the actor has things to express.

GET THE DIME

This is an incredible exercise, which I have been using ever since I was in acting class. It is terribly demanding, but the results, if it is successful, are very worth it. It must be done in a class, because the teacher or another person is involved in it. The actor trying to get the dime is told that getting the dime is a matter of life and death, or something as dramatic. The reason it's called the *dime* exercise is that when I was first introduced to it you could make a phone call for a dime. These days you would have to call it the fifty-cent exercise! What the teacher or facilitator tells the actor who is trying to get the dime might be something like this: "Your wife or girlfriend has just been hit by a car, and she is on the street bleeding, and you need to call an ambulance." Of course, the actor must supply his own intense need in order to get the dime. I have done this one countless times, and I only surrender the dime if the actor convinces me that he desperately needs it. By the time he reaches that state, if indeed he succeeds, he is usually bereft, sobbing, pleading for it. All he can say is that he needs the dime, period.

Example:

"I need the dime. Please give it to me!" The teacher must be resolute in hanging on to the dime until the actor reaches the desired emotional state. "Please, please, I need it. Give it to me!"

As the exercise proceeds, the actor may get angry, hostile, hurt, belligerent, and threatening, but he must never make physical contact with the teacher. At various times in my teaching career, I have told the more aggressive actors in my class that we were separated by a thick wall of heavy glass.

The actor continues: "I need the dime. I mean, I really need it. Give it to me, damn it! I need it. Do you get it?"

The teacher might say, "I don't believe that you really need it. I get that you want it, but I'm not experiencing your desperate need for it." Often in my class an actor might do this exercise three or four times before being successful. When he does succeed in getting the dime, it really is an enormous emotional breakthrough. As it is with all emotionally expressive exercises, repeating this one frequently ultimately eliminates the block to emotional expression.

Accuse and Indict has already been described (in the section on fears), as has the ***Terrific Trio*** (in the section on tension). They are both very useful in this area also.

DUMPS

Somewhat like Vesuvius, but done in a less volatile and depurative frame, this exercise is a way of giving yourself permission to *dump* in public all your less-than-acceptable feelings. Because of its nature and the desired result, it must be done in a group. The actor gets up in front of the group and proceeds to dump all of his incubated thoughts and feelings.

Example:

"I'm sick of being careful around people. I swallow so much shit that I have become a shit swallower, and I'm sick of it! I am going to tell people what I think and what I feel instead of smiling and suppressing emotions that I think they won't like. Fuck you, George! You little prick, you think you know everything about everything, and I've let you get away with your bullshit as long as I'm going to, get it? *(Looking at one of the people in the group.)* And you, Carrie, I have tried to be a friend to you, but you are a stuck-up bitch, who thinks that just because a guy talks to you he wants to get into your pants. Well, big flash for you, Carrie, I am not in the least attracted to you. I hate the cliquishness in this class—small groups that stick together and wear an invisible sign, Keep out! Agents are full of shit. They look at you like you are a piece of meat, and if they don't see dollar signs hanging off you, they don't give you the time of day. I had an agent once who, when I saw him in his office or at lunch, spent the whole time talking about his more successful clients. That's bullshit! *(Looking at the teacher.)* I think you are a good teacher, and I have gotten a lot from you and the class, but sometimes I think you get preoccupied and spaced out. I believe that at those times you lose interest in teaching us."

If this exercise is done in an accepting environment and is responded to benevolently, the actor's confidence expands and he feels more open about expressing his feelings publicly.

THE POWER PREPARATION

This exercise has already been described in the section on physical blocks. It is a very good technique for elevating the ego state and also a very good exercise for expurgating large emotional impulses in a specific area. Because it is expurgatory, it helps to promote expressive confidence. The actor can repeat the process many times until he feels full of power, emotion, and energy.

INGESTATION

Refer to the section on physical blocks for a description of this exercise as well.

IRRATIONAL TANTRUM

Approaching the exercise arbitrarily and in an abandonment framework, the actor begins to explode in an irrational way, almost like a child kicking and pounding on the floor, expressing impulsive irrational expurgations. The content of the expression can be anything, as long as it is large and irrational. I already gave an example in the section on social blocks and obstacles.

INTELLECTUAL INSECURITIES

Many people suffer from the feeling that they are limited intellectually. Quite often this insecurity exists in people with a good education. In many cases it is possible that a person has a very high IQ but that because of psychological damage and abuse, he or she feels limited in intelligence. This area of insecurity can plague one for an entire lifetime, distorting and limiting his sense of self and his ego. If an actor suffers from this area of insecurity, it can limit his ability to understand dramatic material, character development, and the exploration of choices that address the responsibilities and obligations of the character, as well as the relationships and behavior of the other characters in the piece. Sometimes this insecurity is the result of a lack of education, of curiosity, and of the personal acquisition of knowledge and information.

I knew an actor who was fairly successful in his career. He did films, was on a long-running television series, and had made enough money in his career to be able to buy a string of race horses. I knew him for many years. In one conversation that we had he proudly boasted of never having read a single book from cover to cover. I remember being shocked by his admission and wondering how he had gotten through school or if indeed he had ever gone to school. Unfortunately, the only characters he ever played were somewhat Neanderthal, limited intellectually and verbally. I'm not sure that he suffered from any intellectual insecurity, but I believe he should have!

My case was quite different. For many years I was plagued by this insecurity. I actually believed I was intellectually limited, and I suffered greatly at the hands of an older brother who called me a moron throughout my formative years. I experienced the same thing from my grade-school and high-school teachers. My seventh-grade teacher wanted to hold me back because she thought that I was intellectually retarded and should learn a menial trade, where I could work with my hands and ultimately support myself. My intellectual limitation had an emotional origin. I was made to feel stupid by my older brother, and because I was the baby of the family with siblings very much older than I, I felt I could not compete or measure up to them, so I made myself incapable of competing. If I didn't know something, I could not be held responsible for it, so I created a state of intellectual limitation. I suffered greatly through grade school and high school. Instead of taking regular English classes, I had to be in a remedial reading class designed for students who had limited reading and vocabulary skills. I had to go to summer school in order to graduate from high school, and instead of graduating with my class, I got my diploma without fanfare or a graduation ceremony where my parents could come and be proud of me. I started junior college, dropped out before the end of the first semester, and got a job in a factory, assembling children's phonographs. I worked alongside my cousin and seemed happy to drink beer and chase women. The same brother who was very responsible for where I was became so embarrassed by having a brother who worked in a factory and was moving through life aimlessly that he got together with my other brother and sent me to a psychologist he had gone to school with. I spent more than a year in therapy and with the help and guidance of the therapist discovered the source of my insecurities and intellectual limitations. Over a period of two months, I took a battery of tests designed to establish my IQ and the level of my intelligence, and I found out that I had a very high IQ, higher than my therapist's. I resumed my education, graduated from a very prestigious university, and was able to overcome my intellectual insecurities. Not everyone is that fortunate. With a lot of help I was able to become aware of my problem, objectify it, and eliminate my intellectual insecurity. (See my book *The Diary of a Professional Experiencer* for a detailed description of those experiences.)

For actors who suffer from this type of insecurity, the first step is to acknowledge that it exists. Most people sweep their fears under the carpet and continue to function the best way they can in spite of the limitations that this kind of insecurity creates. If you suffer from it, after becoming aware and objectifying it, you should ask yourself, What can I do about it? I think identifying the source and origin would be a good first step. If the insecurity has its origin in a lack of education or training, then the antidote is fairly simple.

READING

Start by reading the newspaper every day; become informed. Knowing what is going on in the world will build your intellectual confidence. Read the dictionary. Start with A and stay with each letter until you get to the next one. Building a vocabulary definitely increases confidence, while at the same time it enlarges both your speaking and your writing abilities. When you read or hear a word you don't know, look it up in the dictionary, which is another way of building your vocabulary.

Raise your curiosity about everything. Ask questions about things you don't know. Find people who are knowledgeable in areas you are interested in and ask them questions. Most people love to be questioned about what they know. Read for information and for pleasure. Read the classics. Read everything you can. Find the subjects that appeal to you and get as much information in those areas as you are able.

The insecurity that accompanies intellectual inadequacy often forces people to hide their lack of knowledge or education. That is a major mistake and only promotes the handicap. As I said before, it is important to be able to say *I don't know.* As humiliating as that might feel, it is vitally important for you to make a habit of expressing your ignorance or lack of knowledge about the things you are unfamiliar with or don't know.

Learn to include these words in your repertoire: *how, why,* and *what,* and use them whenever you don't understand something. Once you have identified your limitations in a certain area, find a class in that subject and enroll in it. Suppose you have difficulty reading: Take a class that teaches the proper way to do it, possibly a speed-reading class. If you have gaps in your education in history, science, or classical literature, you can find many adult-education classes in local colleges.

Go to the theater, watch movies, and read books on acting, theater and the origins of theater. Become educated in the field you have chosen to work in. Read interviews with actors' directors. Study the technical aspects of theater and movie making. Become aware of the components that go into the creation of a play or film.

Most people surround themselves with friends they feel secure with and are not intimidated by, but doing so does not stretch your intellect. Do not discard your friends or respect them less, but look for people who are more educated, knowledgeable, or articulate than you and invite them into your life. At first it can be very intimidating; however, if you pursue those people by asking them about themselves, they will most likely invite you into their circles.

When I was a regular on "The New Phil Silvers Show," I spent a lot of time at Phil's home. He and his wife, Evelyn, became my friends, and my wife and I were frequently invited to their home. Many times we were surrounded by famous comedians and actors, who would sit around and throw one-liners at each other. I felt that I was way out of my league, so I sat quietly and listened and absorbed everything, including their histories. It was very enlightening. Many of them were huge stars, such as Jack Benny, Groucho Marx, or Buddy Hackett. All of them were very accepting of me and very willing to share things with me. I learned a lot and will forever be grateful to Phil, one of the kindest men I had ever known.

MAKING USE OF THE COMPUTER

The computer is the conduit to the world, so use it. Google anything you are curious about. Make a list of subjects and find out about them. Go to the map of the world, and explore regions and countries you are unfamiliar with. Pull up the biographies of historic or other famous people, and read about them, their lives and their contributions. Educate yourself in a multitude of areas. As an actor, learn about other actors. Read their biographies; go to imdb.com and pull up the names of those you admire or are curious about.

PSYCHOLOGICAL INSECURITIES

Almost everyone has had psychological issues: instability; addictions; family predilections; depression; a family member with a background of psychotic episodes, Alzheimer's, alcoholism, drug usage; and others. Many of those issues can create fears, blocks and other problems for the actor. The first thing to do, as always, is to identify the problem. Once you focus on the specifics and understand the issue, you are ready to deal with it. Seeking outside objective help is the best option. If you have an addictive personality, you should find a group or a therapist that can help you through the problem. AA and other groups like it have been very successful in helping people to deal with their issues. Quite often a person fears that he or she might have inherited a predisposition for a certain problem. That insecurity can be its own issue. Because most people are too afraid or embarrassed to share their fears with others, they incubate them with the result that the insecurity or fear festers and may become unmanageable. The best thing to do is to talk about it, share it with someone you trust and respect. Very often talking about a problem objectifies it so that it becomes less threatening.

Many actors fear that they are not psychologically strong enough to deal with the profession, and they opt not to pursue their dreams. I have said many times to the students in my classes that almost all instrumental problems can be traced to a lack of self-esteem, ego, self-worth and entitlement. Building a strong ego is a daily responsibility, and there are dozens of exercises that will help you do that. A number of those are detailed in the section on self-esteem and ego entitlement.

INSECURITIES NURTURED BY COMPARISONS

An important obstacle and one that gets in the way of ego and confidence is created when an actor compares himself to other actors, quite often to more successful ones. He gets intimidated by the talent of those stars and their ability to do what they do. Unfortunately he does not realize that the actors he is intimidated by have had a long time and a lot of training and work to attain the ability and confidence they demonstrate on the screen. Take, for example, Jeff Bridges' performance in *Thunderbolt and Lightfoot.* He was really not that good in that role, but after many films and other work, he won the Academy Award for a brilliant performance in *Crazy Heart,* which proves the point that with work and training actors grow. As an actor I was always fearful of the classics. I was terrified by Shakespeare and the language and style of Elizabethan theater. The fact that English children are exposed to Shakespeare in the third or fourth grade and grow up seeing and reading those plays makes an important point. Like most American actors I personally was not exposed to Shakespeare until my third year in high school. I overcame being intimidated, however, by taking several courses in classical theater. Richard Chamberlain, an American actor who played the lead in a television series, "Doctor Kildare," left the United States, went to England to study Shakespearean theater for the better part of a decade, and became an impressive Shakespearean actor.

So the point I am trying to make here is that, first of all, you are unique in who you are. There is no one in the universe like you.

You are on your own mountain, climbing it by yourself. Your obstacles are unique to you and cannot be compared to anyone else's. Your statement to the theater is an individual one, and no one in the world can possibly make it the way you can. Secondly, when you have identified what intimidates you about other actors' abilities, be objective about your limitations and find ways to overcome them, as I did with my fear of classical theater. I trained, explored, and experimented with the language, style and pentameter of the material, and I overcame my fears. I also accepted the fact that I would never be able to do the classics in the same way as Richard Burton or Sir Laurence Olivier.

SELF-ESTEEM AND EGO ENTITLEMENT

This issue is probably the most important in this book. Almost all of the actor's instrumental problems can be traced to the lack of self-esteem and of a healthy ego. It is rare when a person can grow up in our society without experiencing severe damage to his ego. Quite often the criticism is so subtle that it goes unnoticed, but it nonetheless exacts a heavy toll on the person and often remains an obstacle for an entire lifetime. Many people spend years in psychotherapy wrestling with problems that have their root in a damaged ego, and if they are with a good therapist, he or she will recognize the source of many of those problems. Over my years of teaching I have grappled with ego issues, not only as a teacher but as an actor too. I have used and invented quite a number of exercises and techniques to help the actor. All of them work. They enable him to step onstage and function—that is, as long as he has a process he can count on. However, if he has a damaged ego or lifelong self-esteem issues, the following exercises and techniques work only temporarily, and the actor will have to use them every time he works or is up to bat. Fortunately, I have been working for quite some time to develop a permanent antidote, a way to repair the damage, so that the actor can establish a solid sense of self-esteem and entitlement forever. I quite expect that that claim and my process for accomplishing it will raise some eyebrows, but in my long teaching career

I am very accustomed to that. I will describe the technique later in the book.

COUNT YOUR BLESSINGS AND ACCOMPLISHMENTS

You can do this exercise alone or in a group. It is more effective when it is done audibly rather than silently to yourself. Selectively emphasizing all the positive ego elements and not falling into the trap of qualifying what you say, you simply express, in the form of a sharing monologue, all of your God-given attributes and accomplishments.

Blessings

I already gave an example of how to count your blessings in the section on the fear of inadequacy, so refer to that.

Accomplishments

I also talked about accomplishments in the section on fears, but the exercise is used differently here, so the content is not the same:

"I did extremely well in school, graduated with a 3.9 average. So far I have done everything I've wanted to do in my life. I chose to follow an acting career, and almost everything I have auditioned for I got. I have attracted the right kind of people in my life, people I like and who care about me. I have been able to avoid the traps of this business. I don't sleep with anyone to get work, and I'm proud of the fact that every job I have gotten I got on my talent and abilities. I bought a great car and was able to finance it without borrowing money from my parents. I received great reviews for the last play I was in, and the play received a *Dramalogue* award."

As a self-esteem exercise it should be repeated on a daily basis, particularly when you are auditioning or performing.

TAKING YOUR DUE AND STANDING UP FOR YOURSELF

You can do this exercise when you are alone, with another person, or in a larger group, as a sharing monologue to the whole world, as an imaginary monologue to people in your life who are not present, or as a combination of both. It might be a personal issue that you have with another person, or it can relate to your feelings about your standing on the planet.

Example:

"I deserve to be recognized for everything I am and everything I have done. I am special, and I'm letting all of you know it. *(To an imaginary person.)* And you'd better stop avoiding me! You have always been too self-involved to see who I was and am. I know what's inside me, and soon the rest of the world will know it too. I like who I am and I like that I carry my personality into every creative involvement. I can say no when I feel it, without concern for people's judgment. I know that I am special and how deep my core is."

The exercise can go on for as long as the actor has things to say.

VALIDATE AND AFFIRM YOURSELF

This is somewhat different from Counting Your Blessings in that it is bigger, more theatrical, and somewhat like the Rainmaker, which is another great ego exercise. Besides being verbal and larger vocally, it also requires a physical involvement.

Example:

"I got it! I've really got it. *(This expression should be accompanied by an equally flamboyant physical movement, possibly throwing the arms into the air, being bigger than life.)* Look at this body, muscle definition like a Greek statue's, right? That's right. I got it! Look at me! There isn't anything missing! Look at what great hair I have! My voice is unbeatable. Yes, that's right, I feel perfect!"

All during this exercise the actor should be thrusting his arms skyward, jumping, spinning, and doing martial-arts moves if he can.

EVANGELIST OR RAINMAKER

Just like Starbuck in the play *The Rainmaker,* the actor must be big and over the top in his expressions and subject matter. Just as an evangelist promotes religion, the actor must pick a subject he has great passion for, and he should do the exercise in front of a group of other actors.

Example:

In starting this exercise the actor arbitrarily assumes the persona of an evangelist or of Starbuck: "I want you all to listen to me! I'm gonna tell you something you need to hear. So you want to act? So you want to stand on the stage and command attention, right? Well, listen to me, brothers and sisters! You have to believe in the work. You have to commit your life to your passions. And don't fool yourselves! There is no room for bullshit. It has to be real. There isn't any acting allowed here. You have to be one hundred percent honest and real, and your job is to affect and move the audience. You are the chosen ones, because the rest of the world is full of civilians, and they don't know what it means to be an actor, to be blessed by God with the talent to transform the world. There is no greater nobility than to feel emotions and affect people's lives. I want to hear you. Do you believe? Are you willing to experience life on a fantastic level? *(At this point the actor invites the audience to respond, much like a Holy Roller evangelist.)* I want to hear you. Do you believe? Let's all stand up and raise our arms and voices, and let the world hear us!"

Even though this exercise does not come from an organic source, the size and the subject matter often work to suck the actor in and be very inspiring, as well as lifting his ego to a high level and giving him confidence to take the next step in preparing to act.

POLLYANNA

Pollyanna is a mythical optimist, who sees everything through rose-colored glasses and only relates to the things that are beautiful and positive.

I use this exercise for a variety of reasons: sometimes to address an actor who has a tendency to see that the glass is half empty or that the glass is totally empty and also to access the child energies, the magical child. When used to elevate an actor's self-esteem, it provides a permissive state and allows the actor to feel positive about herself and about everybody and everything in the environment.

Example:

Standing onstage in front of the group or in her own living room, the actor starts to speak arbitrarily: "I love this place. As I look around, I see all the beauty of the objects around me. If that piano could speak, it might say that it feels wonderful to be a piano. The air smells so sweet. I love to take deep breaths and feel the air fill my body. I'm so lucky to be alive! I love people. They are all different but beautiful in their own special way. I feel uplifted by the sounds of nature. When I walk in the woods or down the street, the sounds of nature and life are like a symphony, and it makes me feel as though I just had a wonderful meal. I feel full of joy and hope, and I see the love in people everywhere I go. I love the taste of my tears when I cry with joy. When I look out at all of you, I see that you are surrounded by the most beautiful colors, like a rainbow aura."

Quite often I recommend a monologue from *The Fantasticks*. The young girl is a perfect Pollyanna.

SUPERMAN/SUPERWOMAN

Another very large commitment exercise, this one, which I already described earlier, is done very much like the Evangelist, but instead of being directed outside the self, it is totally about the actor doing the exercise. At first he jumps in by using those hackneyed lines: "Faster than a speeding bullet, able to leap tall buildings in a single bound, more powerful than a locomotive," and so on. Then he makes it more personal, continuing to leap high and flex his muscles.

Example:

"I am a superman! I'm super good-looking and super talented. I have genius capabilities. I have a powerful body and can press my own weight on the barbells. I have a super memory. I remember everything I see and read. I am a super lover. Women lust after me. I am irresistible, and I know it. Everything about me is super. I am truly a superman!"

A woman can also do the exercise, which would then be called Superwoman.

ACCEPTING THE ACADEMY AWARD

Every actor I have ever known has practiced his acceptance speech at the awards ceremony, including myself. It is a desired fantasy that almost everyone thinks and dreams about. If an actor really gets into it in front of the group and expresses all of his gratitude for being nominated and winning the award, it works to elevate his sense of self in a positive way, and sometimes that is all that is needed to supply the ego boost that he needs to begin working. I don't think that it is necessary to give an example of the exercise.

THE MAGIC POCKET

This is a highly imaginative approach. It is done by the actor in any venue and simply consists in his imagining that he has something very special in his pocket: a key to a new Ferrari, a million-dollar bearer bond, a contract for a seven-picture deal to star in all of those films, a love letter from a person he has loved all of his life, and so on. Using sense memory to create the feeling of the object will support his imagination, and if he is successful in creating the fantasy, it will help elevate his ego state.

A PROGRESS REPORT

You can do this exercise alone or with other people present. It is dependent on the truth, is done in the framework of a sharing monologue, and can relate to a specific time period or go all the way back to childhood.

Example:

"When I think of where I was just a few years ago, it boggles my mind how far I have come in so many areas. I feel that I'm less self-involved and self-serving, I care so much more for other people, and I now understand my parents, whereas before I resented them. I am so much more conscious and able to understand things that eluded me in the past. I feel like a much better person. I have achieved a positive work ethic and don't resent having to do menial jobs to support myself while I pursue my dreams. I have solved so many of my instrumental problems, and I know that it is a result of the discipline I have acquired. I feel happier inhabiting me and standing on the stage and being more accepting of the problems of others as well as my own."

This exercise can be done repeatedly, on a daily basis if necessary.

IMAGING

For self-esteem purposes imaging can be an enormous tool for elevating the ego. The actor starts the process with sense memory, using all five senses to create a self-aggrandizing fantasy. Depending on his normal fantasy life, he can create himself in any environment, surrounded by people of all kinds. He can create a casino in Monte Carlo, being specific to create the other rich, opulent people dressed to the nines and dripping in diamonds. Looking at himself in the mirror, he is wearing a four-thousand-dollar suit and a twenty-five-thousand-dollar Rolex wristwatch. He is tanned, and his hair is perfect. He is sitting at a baccarat table with an enormous stack of hundred-thousand-dollar chips in front of him.

Or he can image himself sitting at a table in a conference room at a major motion-picture studio across from Steven Spielberg, discussing the leading role he will be doing in Spielberg's upcoming film.

Or he is lying on his veranda in his house in Hawaii, looking at the ocean and being pampered by three beautiful women catering to his every wish.

Or he is standing on the stage in front of two thousand people on their feet applauding him.

All of the fantasy images must be created so that the actor really experiences the sounds, the odors, and the visual and tactile elements.

SELFLESS INVOLVEMENT

In the section on tension I briefly mentioned Observe, Perceive, and Wonder, which is a technique that can be used for many purposes. When I get to the section in this book about compensational behavior, I will describe in detail how to do that exercise. In the meantime there are other ways to get out of yourself and become involved in the external stimuli. Selfless involvement is the enemy of tension and self-consciousness, and it can free the actor to acknowledge his sense of self and liberate his ego. Elevating his curiosity is a way of getting selflessly involved. Just looking around the place he is in and stimulating his awareness and curiosity of all the objects there can take him out of himself. So many techniques and exercises can be used to address a variety of instrumental and craft issues.

PERSONAL POINT OF VIEW

I already explained this exercise in the section on emotional insecurities. It can also be used as a way to get selflessly involved and clear an ego path. Out loud by himself or in front of the group, the actor just asks himself in a stream-of-consciousness fashion how he feels about everything that comes up.

Example:

"How do I feel about just standing here? I feel like I have to be doing something. How do I feel about being looked at by all those people out there? I have mixed feelings about that. I like the attention, but it makes me a little nervous. How do I feel about this place? I like it. It feels like home in a way. How do I feel about the silence? I don't know how I feel about that. How do I feel about listening to my own voice? I like the sound of my voice. I get a lot of compliments on my voice. How do I feel about Joyce sitting in the first row and studying me? I think she's attractive, and I like looking at her. How do I feel about doing this exercise? I feel more involved than when I started it."

KEEPING A SELF-ESTEEM JOURNAL

One of the books I plan to write in the future is called *An Actor Journalizes*. It is about the seven journals an actor should keep—much like keeping a daily diary. One of those journals is a self-esteem journal. Each day the actor should make an entry about anything that has happened that day that creates good feelings about himself, such as things he discovered, things that people said to him, a rewarding telephone conversation, something that he might have done to help someone, an acting accomplishment—whether it was performing, auditioning, or just the discovery of a great choice he can use for a scene he is doing in his acting class. Each date should be noted at the top of the page, and all the entries should be listed daily and read at the end of the day, and all seven days should be read and reviewed at the end of the week.

TWO-PERSON VALIDATION WORKOUTS

You might just do this exercise with a friend over an afternoon lunch or do it in a class situation. Two people sit facing each other, and in the framework of ordinary conversation they validate each other from a real place. The technique is not arbitrary or imposed. It has to come from an authentic place, from real feelings the two people have for each other. Since it is an exercise and would probably not happen in a normal conversation, one must make a decision to do it, and both people have to selectively emphasize the positive and validating feelings that exist between them.

Example:

HE: You know, I think you're beautiful, and not only on the outside but inside too.

SHE: Thank you. I really like spending time with you. Whenever I leave, I feel that I walk away with so much more knowledge. You are really smart.

HE: It's really easy to relate to you. Most people don't listen the way you do.

SHE: I know that you find me attractive, and I enjoy that, but when we relate, I never feel that there is an underlying agenda. You are very honest.

HE: You know I have learned a lot from you. This is not a one-way relationship.

SHE: I know that. Time really flies. I look at my watch and two hours have passed, and it seems like a fraction of that time!

HE: Thank you for remembering my birthday. I loved the song you sang to me when you called.

SHE: I like working with you. When we rehearse our scene, you spend all the time working—no bullshit.

HE: I'm serious about acting, and I know that you are too.

The exercise can go on for as long as the actors are comfortable doing it.

AFFIRMATIONS

This is done like a daily mantra, or at least it should be. Each sentence should start with "I deserve" and continue with what you want and deserve. There is a good book about affirmations entitled *I Deserve Love* by Sondra Ray. It has many suggestions about the multifarious affirmations a person can do.

Example:

I deserve to be happy. I deserve to be successful. I deserve love and to feel love. I deserve for people to see who I am. I deserve for my talent to be recognized. I deserve to make a lot of money. I deserve to have the things in life I want. I deserve a happy life without struggle. I deserve to have the right people in my life. I deserve to have a loving relationship and a soul mate. I deserve to be healthy of mind and body.

You can vary the affirmations and add other words besides I deserve, such as, *I am accomplished. I have succeeded to get some of the things I have worked for. I am accomplished in a variety of areas,* and so on. If you do this daily and several times each day, you are actually feeding those statements into your unconscious, and over a period of time you will begin to really believe the things that have been input there and, as a result, will elevate your ego and self-esteem to a much higher level.

There are many other exercises that can increase the actor's self-esteem. The ones I have listed can be used as needed, depending on the status of the actor's ego in a specific situation.

REPAIRING THE DAMAGE

All of the ego and self-esteem techniques I have listed and described work to free the actor to function and be creative. However, the damage we experience and suffer from may last an entire lifetime, and while all of the techniques for dealing with ego issues can temporarily address and antidote them, the real problems and the results of having been seriously damaged remain locked up in the unconscious. Depending on whatever specific event or creative responsibility presents itself, quite often the component parts of the experiences that caused the damage will be liberated from the unconscious into the conscious area, stimulating insecurity, fear, and a lack of self-confidence. It is like living with a chronic psychological disorder that, if left untreated, never goes away but instead grows older and more implanted as we age.

I have created a number of techniques and approaches that I really believe succeed in repairing the damage permanently. Having worked with them personally, I have experienced the results. So much of the process is dependent on reprogramming the unconscious. In my book *Acting, Imaging and the Unconscious,* I describe in detail how to use imaging to access the unconscious and input information that relates to already existing unconscious content, changing what the unconscious has stored by replacing it with new material. Carl G. Jung said that the language of the unconscious is images, so using images and imaging has a direct impact on the unconscious.

The first approach and probably the most significant in being able to influence the unconscious is to recall and identify a very memorable damaging experience or event. Once you recall it and remember the component elements, you then re-create it using imaging with sense memory. You hopefully are specific enough to re-create the time, place, people involved, sounds, odors and temperature, as well as everything else you can recall. You start the process by asking sensorial questions that are responded to by the sense you asked the question of, and then you slowly sneak into the imaging process called imaging sensations, which only means that if you ask visual sensory questions, such as, *What do I see when I look straight in front of me? How tall is the person standing there?* all of them are responded to with your eyes, but at the same time all the senses should respond simultaneously: You should smell the odors in the environment, hear the sounds, feel the breeze on your face, and even be aware of what the tastes are in your mouth. As you re-create the experience and are affected by the impact of the content, allow yourself to express your emotional responses. Once you have completed that process, take a few minutes to settle yourself down and then start to re-create the experience a second time; however, this time start to change the component elements, making them positive, affirming, nurturing, and in every area just the opposite of the original. You change not only the elements of the experience but also its final outcome. In order to reprogram the unconscious relationship to the event, you must do this repeatedly over a period of time. How long? That depends on how the reprogrammed experience affects you and on whether you have let go of the original one. We can recall many of the most impacting events, but there are some that we can't remember for a variety of reasons, perhaps because they happened so long ago or because we were so injured that we have protected ourselves from the memory. You should start working with the ones you can recall and then do some choice hunting to unearth the others. I have used choice hunts for the purpose of remembering and discovering new choices for my work as an actor, and I periodically start one of my classes with a choice hunt. I also encourage my students to do it frequently. In this case where we want to look for and find the most damaging experiences, choice hunting is a good approach.

CHOICE HUNTS

You can start at any age. Most people have difficulty remembering anything at very young ages. One of the perks of frequent choice hunting is that it progressively opens up more and more memory banks. When I ask my students to do it as an exercise in my class, I usually start them at five years old. If they can't recall anything at that age, I ask them to go to whatever age they can remember things at.

Example:

I'm five years old, and I am playing in the backyard with my toy fire truck. I hear my mom cooking in the kitchen. She is singing. I'm five years old, and I have to sleep with the light on, because I'm afraid of the dark and the monsters in the closet. I'm five years old, and my pa comes into my room and kisses me on my forehead, and he tells me that there aren't any monsters in the closet, and he opens the closet door to show me. I still think that they are there hiding behind my clothes... (At any point when you run out of memories you move on to the next age.) *I'm nine years old, and I'm in fourth grade, and my teacher is Miss Bloom. I hate her. She is awful. If you agree with what she says, she tells you not to be so agreeable. I can't win with her. She humiliates me in front of the other students all the time, calling me stupid. "Can't you do anything right?" she asks. I'm nine years old, and I'm so upset that I throw up on my desk, and she tells me that I'm a baby and should go home to Mommy. The janitor comes with his red sawdust and cleans the vomit off the desk. I feel that I want to shrink into the crack on the floor.*

As I do this choice hunt, I realize that my experience with Miss Bloom affected my entire primary-school experience and even carried into my high-school years. My confidence was seriously affected and probably in some subtle ways it is still affecting my life. So I am going to use it as an example of how to address an experience and repair the damage.

RE-CREATING THE EXPERIENCE

Since I am really affected by just recalling the experience, maybe I can just re-create it, changing the content—Miss Bloom's behavior and how she related to me—and infusing it with positive behavior, nourishing comments, and benevolence.

I start imaging being in that schoolroom, asking sensory questions about the room, the color of the walls, the picture of George Washington hanging over the teacher's desk. Everything looks bigger because I'm smaller, and I sensorially accommodate for that with my imaging process, using imaging sensations. At a specific point I stop asking questions and just allow all five of my senses to create all of the elements of the experience. In demonstrating the process I have to say what I see, hear, feel, taste, and smell in order for the reader to understand that this is done sensorially, but in reality it is done in silence.

Example:

I see the wooden clock on the wall with its bronze pendulum swinging back and forth. I smell this place, and it is a familiar schoolroom odor. I hear the students moving in their chairs and the wood of the desk creaking. The girl in the desk in front of me has brown curly hair and I smell her perfume. I like it. Miss Bloom is sitting at her desk in front of the class. Her hair is all gray and piled high on the top of her head. We are reading from a class book. The room is warm, and the wool sweater I'm wearing is itching right through my shirt. Miss Bloom looks up and asks us to pay attention, and she calls on me to stand up and read a paragraph out loud. As I stand, she smiles at me with a very approving look and asks me to read. After I finish reading, she tells me that I read very well and that she is very impressed with my reading skills. When she catches my eyes, she always gives me a kind smile, and she asks me how I'm feeling when I walk into the room. Last week she told me that I have the most beautiful blond hair. I look up and see those institutional white globes above my desk, and I remember my mother's voice in the kitchen. Miss Bloom notices that I'm staring at the globes and obviously daydreaming. Instead of berating me she asks, "What are you thinking about, Fred?" (My real name is Fredric. I later changed it to Eric.) *I'm startled but unafraid, and I tell her I was hearing my mother singing in our kitchen. She smiles and tells me how wonderful it is to think about my mother like that and that she wished more children were like me.*

It is very important to know that all of my description is not verbal and that I am creating everything I wrote sensorially and internally. When working sensorially using imaging, the process is much more specific and inclusive than what I wrote above in the description.

To actually be able to repair the damage, I must repeat the re-creation of the altered event many, many times. It can vary in content somewhat, but it must always be affirmative, positive, and the opposite of the original experience. Even though this event occurred many years ago when I was nine years old, it is solidly implanted in my unconscious, and there is no way to know in how many ways it has influenced my life.

Other examples have to do with my brother. I had a psychologically abusive older brother, who was always criticizing and humiliating me, and I must say that probably the most damaging experiences I had were a result of his treatment of me.

I was at his house one time when he had a group of his writer friends over. They were all sitting around and talking literature, plays and movies. I was about twenty-three years old, maybe somewhat older, but junior to all the people there. I was just listening and observing, and I didn't say anything but was enjoying the conversations. At one point one of the men turned to me—probably because he felt that I should be acknowledged—and he asked me if I had read a certain book, at which time my brother Morrey said, "He doesn't read. He is illiterate." That statement was so impacting that I could feel the blood rushing to my head. I felt awful, humiliated, and embarrassed, and I wanted to evaporate. I got up and left the room. I went into one of the bedrooms and sat on the bed. Bernie Gould, one of my brother's longtime friends, came in and said to me that what my brother had done was awful and that he was a *shmuck* for saying that. Bernie apologized for him, and it made me feel only a little better. That experience, coupled with a few other similar ones at the hands of my brother, really damaged me and affected my self-esteem and confidence for many years. To this day I feel the effect of many of those experiences. If I were to use that one and attempt to change its content and outcome, I would approach it the same way as the one about Miss Bloom. Using imaging as an approach technique, I would totally re-create the environment—my brother's living room, the furniture, the height of the ceiling, the odors of the room, the people in it and how they were dressed, the light sources, the sound of the conversations, my brother, how he looked, his body language and the sound of his voice, the attitudes of the people, the feeling on my back from the chair I was sitting in—and the entire experience. Once I had done that, I would re-create it, changing mostly the damaging part and also creating more positive involvements from the people in the room. Here again I would have to repeat the exercise often, probably over a period of time.

Example:

Working to re-create the experience and changing the original to the altered one, I would approach it completely sensorially. Using all five senses simultaneously, I begin to re-create the environment, including every sensory involvement and creating the room, the people, my brother, adding more light to the room, working sensorially to create a happier environment and to adjust the behavior and attitudes of the people for a more uplifting ambience in the room. I work to have many of the people there relate to me more than in the original experience, and when I get to the part where I'm asked about whether I have read a certain book, I say, "No, I haven't," and my brother says, "I have that book, Fred, and I'll loan it to you." Speaking to the group, he continues talking about me: "You know, my brother Fred is a graduate of Northwestern University, and he is out here to pursue an acting career; and having seen him work a couple of times, I must say that he is quite talented." In re-creating the experience, I change my brother's demeanor completely. He becomes supportive and loving, and even as a result of having worked with the experience just once, I feel somewhat different towards him.

Another experience I had with my brother is one I wrote about in my last book. It was extremely damaging to my self-esteem, confidence and belief in myself, and the damage lasted for years. When I started to experiment with the event, attempting to repair the damage, I realized that even though it had become less impacting over the years and as a result of my professional success, I still felt hurt and quite strongly affected by it.

I was on Christmas break from school and had gone to New York to visit Morrey, whose professional name was Edmund

Morris. He was in New York writing for television and the theater. He, his stepdaughter Susan, and I took a trip on the Staten Island ferry. At that time I was going to study photography and had sent applications to various photography schools. I had been interested in shooting pictures ever since my brother Phil had given me a thirty-five-millimeter camera, and I was very serious about a photography career. I had read all of the books and magazines on that subject and was excited about my future. Susan let me borrow her ten-dollar Brownie camera, and I took pictures of the Statue of Liberty from the deck of the ferry. The statue was quite far away and was very small in the viewfinder. A couple of days later we picked up the pictures at a drugstore on a busy New York street. We were standing on the sidewalk as my brother opened the envelope the pictures were in and started to yell at the top of his voice: "What the hell is this? These are by far the worst pictures I have ever seen! You call yourself a photographer? They show no talent, no imagination. Give it up, son, you have absolutely no talent!" I stood there speechless, while everyone who passed by looked at us. I was so embarrassed and devastated I did not touch a camera for ten tears after that incident. Needless to say I gave up all my ambitions to be a photographer, and when I left New York I felt as though I had been beaten up with a whip. Even in recalling the experience I still feel hurt by it, and to this day I really can't say exactly how it damaged me, but in working to reprogram it in my unconscious I do feel it is less impacting.

Example:

Having worked with the experience countless numbers of times, I start pretty much at the same place each time, on the deck of the ferry. I image everything that I remember of that event, and I re-create taking the pictures and sensorially create even the minute elements of the environment: the temperature, the color of the water, the wind blowing in my face, the sounds of people moving around and talking; and then I jump to standing on the sidewalk with the envelope in my brother's hand. At that point I change the content of his behavior and attitude. He says, "Well, my boy, I understand that you took this with a cheap camera, but I must say I like the different angles you shot the statue from. It kind of gives character to the 'Lady.' I would imagine that if you had a telephoto lens the image would be much larger, but these are great! Keep taking pictures! I would like to keep these, Fred, OK?" The strange reality is that if it had really happened that way, I would have pursued being a photographer, and I would not have become an actor, teacher, and writer. In a sense my brother, without realizing it, did me a great favor!

Another incredibly damaging experience happened when I was in the seventh grade. I was attending a grade school directly across the street from my house. It was a four-room schoolhouse that was somehow attached to a larger school several miles away. The larger school was named Key Clark School, and our little school was called Key Clark Branch. I was twelve years old and in grade seven A. My teacher, Miss Lane, was a post-menopausal woman in her middle fifties, with gray hair and a generous amount of facial wrinkles. Actually, she wasn't like my earlier teacher, Miss Bloom, at the other school I had attended. She was much more soft-spoken and not harsh. I was having difficulty comprehending a lot of the work, which I attribute to my terrible experiences with Miss Bloom. John Graef sat at the desk right in front of me and was very helpful in passing back to me the answers to many of the tests. I really feel in retrospect that I was emotionally damaged, not slow in comprehension. Because the school was so small, we had two grades in the same classroom, sixth and seventh. When it was time to move into the eighth grade, it was approved that the twelve students in my grade would all skip grade eight B and go straight from seven A to eight A. At that time Miss Lane approached me and told me that she was going to hold me back and not let me skip the grade, which meant that I would not graduate from grade school for at least one more semester. I was crestfallen. I went to talk to her after class and pleaded with her not to hold me back. She sat in that stiff-back wooden chair, and she said to me, "Fred, I'm sorry, but you are intellectually retarded and you have to stay in grade eight B. Hopefully that might help." I went home crying and told both my brothers, who were still living at home, what had happened, what she had said to me. They were incensed and told me that they were going to speak, not only to her, but also to the principal of Key Clark School, which they did. A short time after that, Miss Lane asked me to stay after school. She told me that she was going to skip me with the others "on trial" and only if I agreed to go to a technical high school rather than to the regular high school in our district. "Fred," she said, "you must learn a trade, to work with your hands, so that when you get older you will be able to support yourself. You are intellectually limited and will not be able to keep up with the others at high school." So I agreed to take a technical course in high school. That is another story, which I won't get into here.

I am sure that that experience colored my years of education with so much insecurity and fear that I only began to overcome it in college after a couple of years of psychotherapy. It was many years later that I started to address it. I worked at first to modify it with imaging, and finally, as my knowledge grew, I started to alter the event and repair the damage. Here again I used sense memory, moved into imaging, and re-created the entire experience with Miss Lane. I changed the content of her behavior and what she had said into a much more benevolent and supportive scenario and created a nurturing relationship. I repeated the process many times and realize, as I am writing this, that my whole attitude has softened. I no longer have any hostility towards her and even begin to understand her motives for her behavior.

The experiences I cited were all real and personal. I used them because I had done work on repairing the damage. The following examples, on the other hand, were contributed by a few of my students, whose names I have changed to preserve their privacy. In each case I am going to relate the original experience verbatim. I will detail it and suggest the process by which the person involved might repair its damaging effects.

This experience was contributed by a woman in my class whom I will call Sarah (not her real name):

"I recall a traumatic incident that happened when I was a little girl and that probably damaged me for years afterwards. I was six years old at the time and in first grade. Our teacher, Miss Sophie, was an ugly, middle-aged spinster, who ruled all the kindergarten and first-grade classes with an iron hand. I think even the other teachers were afraid to stand up to her. We used to make fun of her behind her back because of her strange hairdo and the fact that she wore socks over her stockings; but everyone feared her, and to this day those of us who went to that school still comment about how much damage she did to all of us. For the slightest infraction she would make a child stand for hours in the corner behind the piano. I don't think I ever saw her smile or say a nice thing to anyone.

"Before I left for school on the day I am referring to, my mother had given me a small bag of confetti to take with me. She had told me that since it was Mardi Gras, it would be fun to throw the confetti on some of my fellow students at recess. Once in school I hesitated to do what she had said. I was a shy little girl and was reluctant to stand out from the crowd, as none of the other children were throwing confetti. On the other hand, since my mother had instructed me to do it, I did not want to chicken out either. Recess was almost over and I only had a few minutes left to act, so I finally took courage and threw some confetti on one of the little boys in my class. Unfortunately, just as I was doing so, the bell rang. The boy on whom I had thrown the confetti got upset with me and reported me to Miss Sophie, accusing me of having thrown confetti at him while we were lining up to get into the classroom. Since she thought I had done it after the bell rang, she decided I should be harshly punished. She dragged me to the second-grade class and in front of all the older children told the teacher there that I had been a bad girl and had to be punished. She instructed me to sit under the teacher's desk and not to move from there for the entire period.

"I felt extremely humiliated, especially since she had berated me in front of the older children. I imagined that they were all laughing at me, but there was nothing I could do about it. I had always been good in school, had never been punished before, and was indignant at the unfairness of the punishment. I hadn't done anything wrong! I had thrown the confetti before the bell rang, during recess, which was allowed; but even if I had done it after the bell rang, it wasn't such a horrible thing to do after all! I couldn't say anything, however, because Miss Sophie would probably not have believed me, and, besides, who would have dared to question her judgment anyway? I was so upset by the whole incident I never told anyone about it until I was an adult. I didn't want to tell my mother because I knew she would make light of the whole thing and tell me it 'wasn't important,' which would negate my right to my feelings and humiliate me even more.

"I think the incident traumatized me for the rest of my life. It made me even shyer than I had already been and reluctant to do anything out of the ordinary that might make me incur punishment or ridicule. For a long time I also disliked that second-grade teacher, even though she was a nice person, because she had been witness to my humiliation and hadn't done anything to prevent it. For years afterwards, I felt she was laughing at me every time I saw her. I realized later on, of course, that she herself had probably been afraid of Miss Sophie. In class I was always very quiet and only spoke when called on by the teacher. I rarely even raised my hand because I was afraid I would give the wrong answer and be yelled at or made fun of, even though most of the time I knew the answers. Most of my life I have always been afraid to take any initiative, and I waited for others to lead the way. I think the experience also damaged me in my relationship with men. After that little boy had ratted me out, I always felt that boys, and later men, were not to be trusted. I always think they are going to betray me and am very careful not to make them angry at me. I have always been in relationships with men who trampled all over my feelings, and I am always the one who ends up getting hurt."

This story made me think of my own experiences with Miss Bloom. Grade-school and even high-school teachers can have a devastating impact on our lives, and I wonder if there is any way to screen teachers to determine if they are qualified to influence children, whom they can possibly damage for a lifetime.

REPAIRING THE DAMAGE OF THIS EXPERIENCE

Since the experience happened when Sarah was only six years old and in the first grade, it would be necessary for her to be able to go back to that time and place. If she was a trained actress, she could approach re-creating the experience from that six-year-old place by doing affective memory, re-creating all of the components of that time and place and every element of the environment. Since that prospect is unlikely, she would need to get a sense of the time and place by using imaging. A number of imaging techniques can be used to re-create experiences, all of them described in great detail in my book *Acting, Imaging and the Unconscious.* Sarah could start by asking specific sensory questions or, if using mental imaging, by visualizing the environment, suggesting the components, and encouraging all five of her senses to support the visualization and suggestions. Another approach would be to use story imaging, a process of imaging that runs like a story from the beginning of the experience right through to the end, again supporting everything by responding with all five senses. The third option would be verbalized imaging, which consists simply in verbalizing all of the components of the experience out loud, following the story line. In any case the goal is to create the modified experience so that the original one is relived with positive elements and outcomes. Starting in the schoolyard where they were in recess, Sarah could ask sensory questions related to the environment, the weather, the other children around her, and the sounds and odors she was experiencing. All of those questions would be responded to by her senses through the imaging process.

Example (using story imaging):

How am I dressed? (Responding sensorially to her dress.) *What is the color of my coat? How does it feel on me? What is the temperature? How close am I standing to the boy next to me? What does he look like? How tall is he? Where are the other children? What does the ground look like, feel like? How close is the door to the classroom?* (All of these imaging sensory questions are responded to sensorially.) *How loud are the voices of the children close to me? What are they saying? I'm holding the bag of confetti. What color is it? What does it feel like in my hand? I'm afraid to throw the confetti, but I'm going to do it. How does it feel in my hand as I take it out of the bag? What is its texture as I move it around in my hand? As I throw it at the boy nearest to me, it hits him in the face and sprinkles into his hair. He begins to laugh, grabs the bag, and throws the rest of the confetti at me. I laugh, and so do all the children around. I hear the bell ring. What does it sound like? How does it make me feel? As I enter the room, I see Miss Sophie looking at us. She seems curious about the confetti in our hair and on our faces. She smiles and asks us to take our seats. She remembers it is Mardi Gras and says something about the holiday. She calls me to her desk and asks me about the confetti, and I tell her that my mother gave it to me and told me to sprinkle it at recess. She laughs and pats me on the shoulder, and I go back to my seat. We pick up our books and start to read what is on the page. It is quiet and pleasant in the room, and I realize how much I love school and learning.*

Every part of the event must be experienced through the senses. Even when one uses mental imaging and suggests all the elements of the story, the responses must be approached through all five senses. The environment and all of its components must be very specific. The people involved must be re-created in great detail—the way they looked, the color of their hair and eyes, the shape of their faces, the sound of their voices, whatever odors they emitted, their actions and body styles, and the clothing they wore. It is also very important that the imaging process be done on a here-and-now basis rather than retrospectively. The sensory-imaging questions should be phrased as if the event were happening now.

If the process is repeated many, many times over a fairly long period, the re-created experience will replace the original one in the unconscious and will ultimately repair the damage caused. Of course the re-creation will not be able to rectify all of the growing-up experiences that were influenced by the original event; however, you will establish a totally different relationship to the original, which will change the way you feel about it. From this point forward it may cease to affect you in a negative way.

The next experience was contributed by "Adrienne":

"At eight years old I began experiencing episodes of severe depression. By twelve years old I was cutting myself. I couldn't understand the pain I felt inside, so by matching that pain with a wound that I could see, identify as something that hurt, and have the ability to bandage up and watch heal, I felt more in control and had a sense of relief.

"Years later as a sophomore in college, I was creating a piece for my choreography class based on the self-abuse struggles I had faced throughout my life. I was very depressed at the time and was fighting my urges to cut. I was doing all that I could and wishing like crazy that I would come out on the other side of depression once again. That was my inspiration. The movements told the story of a girl physically abusing herself but also fighting the aggression where in the end the healthy, peaceful part wins and she walks off the stage glowing with happiness. It was a message of hope. My teacher and the class were touched and loved it.

"After performing it in school, I couldn't wait to show the piece to my mom. The next time I went home to visit we went into her exercise studio, where I put on the music and poured my heart out into the dance. My mom stood against the wall watching me. The music ended as I walked off with the happy glow of hope. I turned to her to see what she thought, and she was speechless. A few seconds passed and she said, as cold as could be, 'That was really disturbing.' Then she turned her back and marched out of the room. I was shocked and mortified that I had shared something so personal and had been rejected by my own mother. I yelled after her 'I'm sorry!' I apologized for exposing her to a part of me that I now identified as unworthy of being seen or being loved. I felt ashamed and humiliated, and from that moment on I put a wall up to protect those I loved from being 'disturbed.' The wall also protected me from the severe pain that I felt as my mom formed that sentence and turned her back on me.

"When I felt down, I isolated myself from the world. In order to survive as an accepted part of my family, I faked happiness when I was sad. I hid feelings that I thought might offend or scare people. It felt so lonely to be hurting and keeping it a secret. My relationships were no longer completely genuine, just involving the sides of me that I thought would be received with love. This translated into my art as well. I wouldn't give myself permission to express a wide range of emotions. All I could access were things such as carefree, excited, loving feelings, etc., the emotions that my mom would have praised. I disowned a huge part of myself, and I really want to own it and express those parts of me again. As an artist I'm missing out on so many colors I want to be creating with. I'm working hard to give myself permission to feel all my feelings, to repair the damage I have experienced, and to glow again."

When I first read Adrienne's experience, I too was shocked and disturbed by her mother's response. I am fully aware how impacting and damaging a single experience can be, especially when coming from someone you love or respect. There is a positive element in that experience and a negative, damaging part. The positive one is the response she got from her teacher and the other students in her choreography class. In re-creating the experience, I believe that Adrienne should spend time with the first part, emphasizing all of the encouraging things said in the class and the emotions of the people involved. When she has re-created all of the elements, such as the music, the dance, and the responses, she could move on to the damaging portion with her mother, re-creating the environment, the music, her mother, and all of the sensory elements that were part of the event—this time, however, changing it into a very positive and encouraging experience.

Example:

I am dancing and interpreting all of my movements to communicate the story of how I am addressing what I have done and how I am modifying it, learning from it and evolving into another level of self-acceptance. (As she images sensorially the music, her movements, and the components of the exercise studio, all of her senses are responding to her re-created images.) *As I twirl around, I catch a glimpse of my mother smiling at me dancing. I feel a wonderful and exciting energy climbing up my body from the floor. I feel as if my feet are just barely touching the ground. As the music ends, I stand there sweating and exhilarated. My mother is glowing with pride, and as she approaches me I see tears rolling down her cheeks. She embraces me with such power I almost lose my balance. "I love you, I love you, I love you, you wonderful, beautiful daughter of mine," she says. "I am so proud of you. I knew you could dance, but I had no idea how well. I love you!"* (All of her expressions must be re-created sensorially, and Adrienne must hear the sound of her mother's voice, see the expressions on her face and her body language. She must re-create the familiar odor of her mother and feel her arms tightly around her.)

If Adrienne re-creates the modified experience many times, there is a very strong possibility that the unconscious will surrender the original and embrace the new input.

This experience was shared with me by a student I will call Myrna:

"I remember the big house we lived in. It was so big that my mom and I had the whole top floor to ourselves. The room I slept in was small. The colors were brown, as were the window frames and the door. The walls were blue. It also had blue curtains. It was a very bright room because it was almost half glass. The entrance door was also made of glass and had a small curtain hanging in front for privacy.

"I remember the first night that it happened. I was in bed trying to fall asleep when I heard my mother's Renault drive away. A little time later Ralph (not his real name) came upstairs. He walked into the bedroom and sat down beside me. I remember everything in detail, and I can tell you that as I am writing this I feel sick to my stomach. He slowly started touching me between my legs and then he smelled his fingers. He told me that he liked the smell. I didn't know or realize what was happening. No one had ever approached me like that. I had no understanding about sex, and the feeling was very new to me.

"Since I didn't have a dad before Ralph came into my life, he was very important to me. I adored him. The feeling wasn't bad. I kind of enjoyed it. It was my first sexual feeling, but of course I didn't know that at the time.

"After that night I felt a bit strange but acted like nothing had happened. I did not tell my mother right away. This happened a couple of times more, always when my mother would leave the house. I remember the odor of alcohol. My mother and Ralph would drink port, but they were never drunk.

"One evening we were lying on the sofa watching TV when he started touching me again. My mother was in the kitchen cooking, and we were around the corner in the living room. It was like a game. She was not supposed to know about it. We did not talk about that, but I felt that was what he expected. It felt nice. I was used to the feeling now, and it was exciting.

"I'm not sure how many times this happened, and I don't remember how I reacted to him, but at a certain moment I realized that I felt this was wrong. My mother and Ralph started getting into arguments, and I could see that my mother was sad and in pain. I think that was the moment when I decided to tell her about what had been happening.

"We were driving away in her Renault, and she asked me if I was OK. I told her what Ralph had done and that I wanted him to stop. We had a 'family' meeting soon after that, and I told him that I did not like what he had been doing and that I wanted it to stop. He promised and never approached me like that again.

"I remember this strange feeling of not being able to express myself, being stuck with this weird guilt and anger, something I could not express to my mother, to whom I could normally express anything.

"We did leave him shortly after that. I never got the whole story, but I'm sure it had something to do with what he had done to me. After about a year and a half my mother got back with him. Ralph was diagnosed with lung cancer, and we moved back into the house. We helped him to recover, and he did recover. They got married. It felt like we would start over again. Six months later he died of liver cancer.

"I guess I felt guilty all my life. I never talked about this in detail with my mother or anyone else. I felt very ashamed, and I repressed my anger, and I think that this whole experience is the source of my inability to express anger. I could never show my anger because I was afraid it would affect and destroy their relationship. So all of my life I have suppressed my angry feelings towards everything and everybody. When Ralph was dying, I held back everything that I felt about the abuse because he was sick. Not only did that experience stunt my ability to express anger, dissatisfaction or criticality, but it also made me wary of men for a good deal of my life. I still have nightmares about the experience."

Myrna's experience is not uncommon. Many children are sexually abused by their parents or stepparents, but that does not minimize the incredible impact, which can last an entire lifetime. It seems that Myrna has very good sensorial recall of the experience and the environment, and she can use imaging to change some of the elements and the entire outcome of what originally happened. Of course, it is not possible to go back through her whole life and change the impact, the relationships and the trauma of her life. No matter how successful you are in repairing the damage, it happened. The purpose of doing these techniques is to help you go on happily from here. By implanting new information into the unconscious on a repeated basis, you replace the original experience with a healthier, happier event. Let us say, for example, that Myrna still has anger and resentment for her stepfather. That incubated emotion can evaporate with changing the experience and implanting a new one. It is important to note that repairing damaging experiences leads to a better quality of life and, in addition, allows a person to be free to act. Myrna has told me a number of times that throughout her acting career she has struggled with being able to feel and express anger and that, whenever she was obligated to that feeling in a piece of material, she had to impose it rather than experience it. In addition, she has struggled with her sexuality in a number of relationships, feeling freedom only when she could be the aggressor. She also has difficulty acting with older men if there is any sex involved in the material. All of those issues can be related back to the story she shared with me.

Myrna is going to start the process of changing the original event into a positive, loving one. Since she has had training in my system, she is much more capable of approaching the modified experience with sensory facility.

Let us say that she elects to use story imaging combined with verbalized imaging and that she starts the process with a combination of sense memory and a verbal sharing monologue, as she follows the continuity of the event through story imaging.

Example:

"I'm lying in bed looking at the ceiling and watching the shadows of the leaves on the trees outside the window dancing and making pictures. I am sleepy but not yet ready to sleep. I love the way this room smells. It is the odor of the wood, me, my mom and the stuffed animals all around me. *(Everything expressed is sensorially experienced by Myrna.)* I hear my mother's car driving away. I'm wondering where she is going, maybe to the market. I feel warm and protected when I think of my mom. I can smell her perfume, as it has settled on everything around me. I feel my eyelids getting heavier. I hear footsteps on the stairs, because the stairs creak when you step on them. *(Everything she describes in the verbalization and all of the sounds are experienced through all of her senses.)* I see the door to my room opening slowly, and in shadow I see Ralph standing in the doorway. He doesn't move, just stands there looking at me. I wonder if he can see me in the dark. I get a very strong odor of him, mixed with a smell of alcohol. I see his silhouette moving towards my bed. He is stepping carefully so he won't wake me. I pretend to be asleep. He sits down on the bed next to me and touches my head, brushing my hair back. I hear him say, 'I love you, little one.' It makes me feel good. I never knew my real father, so Ralph has become my father, and I love him. He is a gentle, loving man. He is very good to my mother. I feel him pull the covers over me. He pats my forehead and whispers, 'Goodnight, sweet little one.' I remember all of the times I have sat on his lap and how he bounces me up and down and we all laugh together as a family."

In addition to repeating this modified experience, Myrna could create other nurturing, healthy ones with her stepfather.

About a year ago "Jonah" started working in one of my classes. He was a young man about thirty, very shy, somewhat introverted, who had difficulty being emotionally expressive in the exercises I gave him. When I asked him to share his life with the class, he told us that he kept to himself a lot and, except for going to work, stayed at home and read books. His face would turn red every time he got onstage, and he had difficulty getting past his self-consciousness. After many instrumentally liberating exercises, he was able to express more of what he felt. He started to bond with some of the other students and to feel less self-conscious on the stage. I could see that he still suffered from the impact of an experience or experiences in his life, but I didn't know what they were. One day in class he shared an experience that he had had when he was five or six years old. He related the event without being prompted. It just came out when he was doing Personal Inventory:

"I was in school, and my teacher was sick, so the principal came in and took over the class. He was an older guy and not used to teaching a class, so he invented some games he thought might be good for us to participate in. He would ask questions of the other students that related to their home life, posing the questions as a test of awareness. At one point he asked, 'Who in this room has a mother that works for United Parcel Service?' He was relating that question to me, but I only knew that my mother worked for UPS. I didn't know that United Parcel Service was UPS. I was five years old! He waited for a moment or two, and when I didn't respond, he said in a very sharp and shrill voice, 'Well, Jonah, it seems to me that you must have swallowed a dumb pill this morning!' All the kids in the class looked at me and started to laugh. I felt like I wanted to be swallowed up by the floor and disappear. He didn't stop there. He went around the room and asked each of the students if they knew where their father or mother worked, humiliating me even further. After that experience I stopped relating to anyone. I kept to myself, and for the rest of my life I avoided contact with kids in school, and when I got older, it carried into every relationship I had. I could do my work as long as I didn't have to be involved personally or emotionally with anyone. It's funny, I haven't thought of that experience for a very long time, but it is so obvious that it affected my entire life."

I'm sure that the memory of that event popped into his head because of his increased awareness prompted by his growth in my class. I told him how to go back and start the repair process.

He should start by re-creating the environment, the classroom and all of the objects and the children there, the principal—where he sat or stood, what he looked like and sounded like, how he was dressed—sensorially re-creating everything he remembers, using imaging sensations to respond with all of his senses at the same time. Once he has created the place and the people, he must accommodate the difference in the size of objects, since he was a small boy. It is necessary to somehow get a sense of being there-and-then on a here-and-now basis. That can be accomplished by actually re-creating as many of the components as possible. If he accomplishes that, he has a direct conduit to the unconscious. At the point where he feels he is in that space, he can start changing the ingredients and the outcome of the original experience.

Example (using verbalized story imaging):

"I see Mr. Anderson standing in the front of the class. He is smiling and looking at each of us with a very open and friendly attitude. He tells us that our teacher is at home with a cold and that he is here to *substitute* for her. I don't understand what that word means, but I like the way he is relating to us. He starts by asking us what our names are, and then he asks each kid something about his home life, what his hobbies are, what he likes about school, and who his friends are; and then he begins to quiz us about the things he already knows about us. When he asks that question about whose mother works for United Parcel Service, he waits for a moment and then says, 'Well, it is also known as UPS.' When I hear that, I raise my hand and I tell him that that is my mother's job and that she has been there for a long time. He acknowledges my answer and smiles at me. He asks me how she likes working there and if she has ever taken me down to her workplace. I tell him that she has and that all the other workers were impressed with me and I had a good time. I can see that some of the other kids seem envious that my mother has taken me to her workplace. All in all it is a very good experience."

If Jonah repeats this a number of times, he should be able to replace the original experience with the amended one. Each time he does this he should re-create the environment sensorially.

THE SECOND-CHANCE EXERCISE

This is yet another approach to repairing or changing the impact of traumatic events. As you recall or find hurtful and damaging encounters with people in your life, you can give yourself permission to revisit those experiences by talking to those people and saying to them what you didn't originally. This constitutes a second chance for you to go back and tell them what you want them to hear, and take your due, stand up for yourself and put them in their place. We all have a slew of such experiences with people, and we incubate the terrible feelings of if only I had said that, or if only I had really let him have it! Those unresolved events, as well as the nagging feelings of unresolved issues, haunt us and are very damaging to our self-esteem. This exercise is approached through *Imaginary Monologues.* Talk to the persons as if they were really there and say things that you didn't in the original encounter. It can be more effective if you sensorially create the persons you are speaking to and allow for their responses; however, the impact of an imaginary monologue is still very effective even if you just imagine the other persons' responses.

Example:

I am going to use a person from one of the above experiences. I am going to talk to Miss Bloom, my fourth-grade teacher, even though I was incapable of saying the things I am about to say to her and she has probably been dead for a long time now.

"You know that the things you say to nine-year-old children, and especially the way you related to me, calling me stupid and embarrassing me in front of the class, are a total result of your unhappy, miserable life. You are an antiquated spinster, filled with the disappointments of an unfulfilled life. You are fat, unattractive, and filled with toxic bile. How is it possible that you can be turned loose on innocent nine-year-old children and undermine their self-esteem? God only knows how many others you have damaged on this unholy journey of yours. There should be a system for catching people like you and taking them out of a position where they can hurt so many children."

I wish I could have said those things to her. A second chance is helpful in expurgating incubated and unresolved issues with people who have been damaging and hurtful to you. Second chance encounters don't have to be negative or hostile. They can contain unfulfilled wishes and the need to communicate love and other such feelings that you didn't express at the time.

The following is an imaginary monologue that has been repeated in my brain as well as having been done as an inner monologue. I lost my son four years ago. He was forty-four and died as a result of complications from diabetes. The loss has been devastating, and my grief is indescribable! I questioned myself as to whether I should share this as a second-chance exercise but decided that it would be as good for me as for the reader:

"I don't know where to start. I have thought many times since you left that we used to communicate about our common interest, automobiles. I know that you loved me, and I loved you beyond description. You were the light of my life, but for some strange and unknown reason we never expressed love to each other directly. When you grabbed my arm and squeezed it until it hurt, I knew it was a mixture of love and anger, and I know that there was resentment there, but when you put your hands on me, I could feel the love you felt, even though you didn't verbalize it. I can't understand why we didn't express it that way. I do remember that sometimes at the end of a telephone conversation I would say, 'I love you, Jeff,' and you would reply with, 'I love you too, Dad,' but what I wouldn't give to sit down with you and tell you how deeply I loved and love you now! I would like to tell you that almost everything I did in my life and work I did with you in mind. I remember walking into your class and standing behind your chair, putting my hands on your shoulders and being so filled with pride about what a wonderful teacher you were. I felt your body under my hands, and I was expressing so much love. Why didn't I tell you that more often?"

I'm not sure how that will affect my unconscious, but I know that with repetition I may start to forgive myself.

THE VERBAL APPROACH

Here is a third way of working to repair the damage. You can do it in conversation with another person or alone in a sharing monologue. If you are talking to another person, you simply relate the experience in the conversation. It is not necessary to tell the original damaging experience, but only the modified repairing version. A conversation is a good way to start the verbal approach, but unless you can repeat it a number of times, you must then work alone in the framework of a sharing monologue, preferably out loud. You must repeat the process a great number of times, keeping the content much the same.

If you tell a lie often enough, the lie becomes the truth, and when you retell it you believe in it as the truth. That is what we hope will happen when reprogramming the unconscious. If you keep inputting the modified content, ultimately the unconscious will accept it as the original experience and will let go of what was originally implanted.

APPEALING TO THE UNCONSCIOUS

By using as many of the techniques as are available, the actor can certainly repair the damage he has suffered over his lifetime. A good way to address the unconscious is to do a sharing monologue just before going to sleep. If you go through the amended experience three or four times before drifting off to sleep there is a strong possibility that it will stimulate a dream or two, and even if it doesn't, you are implanting the experience into the conscious/ unconscious just before the unconscious is awakened by sleep.

Very little is known about the unconscious. Jung was probably the most ardent explorer of it and had more knowledge than anyone, and I believe he said that the unconscious was not evaluative or analytical but just accepted input from our experiences and stored it in all of the unconscious memory banks. My theory about repairing the damage we have sustained is based on replacing old experiences with new ones that have a different content and on reprogramming the unconscious by repeating the process many times, using the language of the unconscious.

Dreams and Dreaming

Since dreams and dreaming are a time when we are most connected to the unconscious, a great deal of reprogramming work can be done by using our dreams to input the altered material through ordering up a dream, dream catching, lucid dreaming, participating in a dream, and so on.

The entire subject of dreams could fill a large bookshelf with books and explorations of the subject. Many "dream masters" out there have devoted their entire lives to the exploration and study of dreams. I have a fairly elaborate section on dreams and how to use them to communicate with the unconscious in *Acting, Imaging and the Unconscious*. For our purpose, addressing the process of repairing the damage, I will concentrate on using dreams as a conduit to the unconscious.

While in bed just before you go to sleep, ask yourself to have a dream about the amended experience you have been working on (ordering up a dream or dream catching). If you go through the experience just before nodding off, there is a possibility that you might have a dream related to it. Hopefully, if indeed you do dream about the experience or the event, the dream will contain its amended version. If that happens, you can be assured that it has been implanted in the unconscious.

Lucid Dreaming

A lucid dream, which I am sure almost everyone has had, is when you are fully asleep and are dreaming but know that you are dreaming and can fully participate in the dream. If the dream is about the experience you are working with, it will be a great opportunity for you to manipulate its content, adding positive elements to the experience and thereby re-creating it with ingredients that will change the original into a much more nurturing event.

The Hypnagogic State

That is the state that occurs just before falling asleep or just before awakening, when one is not fully asleep and the conscious and unconscious are closely connected. Usually you experience bizarre images or fleeting thoughts that don't seem connected to anything understandable. This state lasts only a few seconds but can be very important for connecting with the unconscious. While you are experiencing this phenomenon, you can suggest an impacting image about an event you are working on. It will be like talking directly to the unconscious part of you. This doesn't happen every night or every morning, but if you become aware of the possibility, you can make use of it.

Almost every time I do a repairing the damage exercise in class I get the same question from my students: "Does this mean that if you are successful in changing the experience you lose it as a possible choice?" I always respond with the same answer: "Yes, it is possible that you won't be able to use that experience as a choice in the future, but you have hundreds of other choices that can effectively address a similar obligation. The amended experience supplies a completely new choice possibility, and of course, you do remember the original experience, but after changing it you won't be affected or damaged by it in the way you were."

RESURRECTING THE INNER CHILD

In addition to repairing the damage and to all the other activities you involve yourself in as an actor on a daily basis, you should add some time to free the inner child, opening the doors for it to come out and play. Not only will this activity contribute to your growth as an actor, but it will also elevate the joy and fun in your life. Children are imaginative and willing to believe in everything. As they run around their house riding a broom, they imagine that it is a white horse named Thunder and believe that they are in the middle of the desert being chased by a band of bloodthirsty Indians. It becomes real for them. We are all born with the ability to imagine, pretend and believe, but as the years pass we lose that ability because of social pressures and criticism. For an actor, that is a great tragedy. The disappearance of those abilities makes it much more difficult for him to believe in the circumstances of the material. Experiential acting depends on actually *having* the experience of the character in a scene.

Fortunately the ability to believe and pretend is not gone forever and can be resurrected. To do that the actor must begin a daily process of work. A lot of exercises and techniques stimulate the imagination and encourage one to really believe in something that is not real. All my life I have been playing, fantasizing, imagining and creating a pretend life. It started early for me. I hated going to bed at night and would do almost anything to avoid it. Since I was going to school, my parents always made sure that I was in bed at a certain hour; so in order to accept the bed schedule I would create a fantasy, for example a story about an adventure on a large sailboat crossing the ocean and going around the world. I would experience the thrill of being in new places, meeting all kinds of people, some of whom were dangerous and threatening. I would duel with them, always being victorious in my battles. I would continue the fantasy the next night, picking up where I had fallen asleep the night before. Sometimes an adventure would go on for weeks at a time until I concluded it or grew tired of it, at which point I would create a different one; for example, I would be on a safari in the darkest part of Africa, being threatened by lions and hostile headhunting savages. The heat and my thirst were overwhelming, and I would wake up drenched in sweat. My mother would wonder if I was ill, because the sheets were all wet. I tried to explain, but no one believed me. I did this for many years, adding all kinds of new things to each fantasy.

I also had a grade-school friend, with whom I would play pretend games in his basement every day after school. Those too were episodic. I looked forward to the school bell ending the day of class so I could rush over to John's house to play. John and I were in the Boy Scouts, so it was easy to play army, wearing our uniforms. We cut out cardboard medals and stripes and fought World War II in his basement. At times we were wounded and needed medical care, so we bandaged each other with toilet paper and charged up the beach into combat. I must have killed thousands of the enemy, and I was awarded the highest honors my country could bestow on me. Way before I even dreamt of being an actor, I was playing, fantasizing and pretending. It carried into my high-school years and into college and persists to the present day. As an adult I play all kinds of daily games. When driving my car, I imagine that I am a fighter pilot in a P-51 Mustang, and as I drive through the canyon, on each curve I lower the right wing and bank to the right and then to the left. I am actually driving at a reasonable, legal speed but imagining that I am flying at two hundred and fifty miles an hour. I have been a gun collector for many years. I don't hunt or kill anything, but I am fascinated by fire arms and have a substantial collection. When I watch a movie on television, if it is a western, I strap my single-action colt on my hip and take part in the story, oftentimes drawing more quickly than the movie hero. If it is a war movie, I select the proper weapon to participate in the D-Day invasion. I play with the miniature cars that I have collected over the years. Most of them are sports cars or race cars, so I often create a fantasy about being in a race, the Indianapolis 500 or some other race at Laguna Seca. I'm behind the wheel of my Porsche, taking the curves, downshifting, hearing the roar of the engine as it decelerates, and, as I skid into the turn, smelling the burn of rubber, the odor of gasoline, the perspiration dripping down my goggles. I slip into the straightaway and up shift. The engine roars with power and energy, and my speed increases as I pass four other cars. I'm feeling excitement and a sense of euphoria, as the checked flag drops down right in front of me. I won! I won! I can't describe the intense feeling I have.

As I got older, many of my fantasies turned romantic, and I would imagine being with beautiful, famous women. My pretend games and fantasies had no boundaries. I could go anywhere and do anything. I broke the bank in Monte Carlo; I visited with dignitaries, kings and presidents and advised them on how to run their countries. I must say I believe that if they had taken my advice it would have been to their benefit.

I share my experience with those of you who are reading this just to give you a sense of the things I have been doing that have kept my *magical child* alive and active in my life. In my training as an actor, after I dealt with and eliminated my tension and many of the other obstacles that blocked me from functioning, I was able to use the child energy to help me believe in the choices that I made and experience the emotions of the character I was addressing. I really believe that to be able to realize the full impact of being an experiential actor, you must liberate the inner child, and to do that you must work on techniques and exercises every day to free that part of you from the prison it has been put in while you were growing up. Developing yourself as an actor is a twenty-four-hour involvement three hundred and sixty-five days a year for your entire life. The journey only ends when you die, and, who knows, Lee Strasberg might be up there holding classes! In addition to what you do for yourself, therefore, invite the child back into your life. Here is a list of exercises you can do every day:

REVISITING AND RE-CREATING ENVIRONMENTS, EVENTS, FRIENDS, AND TOYS FROM YOUR CHILDHOOD

Environments

Going back into your childhood, start by recalling the places you lived in—the bedrooms, the backyards, the hiding places—and then sensorially re-create them using all five of your senses. Asking sensory questions in all five senses, attempt to see the rooms, the colors, the wallpaper, the blanket on your bed, the pictures or drawings on the walls, and where the light sources were; smell the odors in the room; experience the tactile feel of the pajamas; and hear the sounds in the rooms, those coming from outside, and your parents' voices as they drifted in from the other rooms. Respond to all of your sensory questions in the specific sense that you are exploring. You must also approach it in the here and now, not retrospectively. It is not "What were the sounds?" but "What *are* the sounds?"

Events

Remembering birthday parties and other meaningful events of your childhood is also very important: kindergarten, a Fourth of July picnic with hot dogs and orange soda, your father taking you to your first circus, your first bicycle with training wheels, being tucked in by your mother and listening to her read stories to you, a family vacation by the lake, learning to swim, the first time your dad took you fishing, watching the shadows play on the ceiling of your bedroom just before falling asleep, etc. Re-creating those events sensorially is very important in appealing to and piquing unconscious responses from that time. With repetition you will elicit a relationship to the inner child, who will begin to participate in your life.

Friends

The friends we had in our early life were very important. It was the beginning of the formation of our social skills. We all had friends that somehow disappeared as we grew older or moved from one place to another. For most of us those relationships were very important: the boy or girl who lived across the street; kids from school we spent a lot of time with and with whom we forged a meaningful relationship, which we looked forward to and that was very fulfilling; friends we shared all our secrets with; the little girl or boy we kissed for the first time behind the garage; and so on.

Start the process of re-creating those people by visualizing them with your inner eye, and then begin to re-create them sensorially with your senses. Make them real to yourself. Attempt to hear their voices and smell their odors, see the mannerisms that are distinctly theirs, their particular smile or the way they laughed, the clothes they wore, the games you played and the places you played in. Go on the trip, and encourage it to take you wherever it will. Allow yourself to feel the specific emotions that come up while you are creating all of those people in your life. You will be surprised that some of the excitement that bubbles up to the surface is a feeling you haven't had in a very long time.

Toys

I remember vividly the toys I had as a youngster. I collected bubblegum cards, which were mostly war cards, since the Second World War was going on. They depicted the Japanese enemy wearing thick, horn-rimmed glasses, with large buckteeth that occupied half of his face. I imagined fighting on those islands and always being a hero. I had a Daisy BB gun, which my brother Phil had bought for me when I was seven and which I could only shoot when he was there to oversee the safety of the situation. On Saturdays and when he wasn't at work, we went across the street to a large empty lot to shoot at targets, and we attracted all the kids in the neighborhood, who would ooh and aah as I hit the smallest targets. They called me Buffalo Bill and Annie Oakley. That is when my love for guns began. I could do something that was received with admiration, and it grew into a lifelong attachment to firearms and shooting accuracy. I loved my Daisy BB gun and often slept with it.

When I was a little older, my father bought me a used bicycle. New ones were impossible to come by, since all the steel was going into the war effort. He paid a fortune for it. Thirty dollars was a fortune in 1943! I loved that bike and rode it every day. We kept it in a shed in the basement of the apartment house we lived in, and when I wasn't riding it, I would check on it two or three times a day to make sure it had not been stolen.

There were many other toys in my life that I treasured. I had toy guns and cowboy holsters, guns that fired caps and made a lot of noise but didn't fire a projectile. I ran around the house and the backyard fighting cattle rustlers and Indians.

I read comic books incessantly and collected them. My favorites were *Superman, Captain Marvel,* and *Daredevil.* Against my bedroom wall were stacks of comics, which contributed to my imagination and the fantasies I created as a result of their impact on me.

As an exercise to stimulate that inner child you should start with remembering all the various toys you had and then begin to re-create them sensorially one by one, using all of your senses. In my case every toy or object I owned developed some kind of personality. Sometimes just the tactile involvement, the odors, or the sounds they made, as well as the way they looked and how each one made me feel, inspired a relationship to each of them. With repetition all of this work will appeal to the unconscious and will take you back to that inner child and invite him or her to join in your life.

In the film *Big* a little boy makes a wish in front of a magical fortuneteller machine. He wishes he were big, and his wish is granted. The boy becomes Tom Hanks. As a little boy in an adult body, Hanks had to retain the child energy, which I think he did very well. In the scene at FAO Schwarz toy store in New York, jumping on that huge piano and delightfully enjoying every moment from his inner-child place certainly makes the point about the need to access the inner child and invite him into our lives so we can use that energy to fuel our acting.

DOING THE THINGS YOU DID AS A YOUNGSTER

When we were little, we really loved going to amusement parks, riding on the roller coaster or the merry-go-round, sitting on a beautifully colored wooden horse as it circled round and round, going up and down to the beat of the music. Even though it might be embarrassing to ride on the carousel as a fully grown adult, it would be fun to do and would constitute a commitment to training as an actor.

Visit toy stores and examine the toys, particularly the ones that remind you of your own childhood. Play with them, and if a particular toy appeals to you, buy it, take it home, and play with it. Go to the circus. I hate the way they treat the animals, so find a circus that doesn't feature animals but has high-wire acts, clowns, crazy antics and cotton candy. Kick the sawdust on the ground and inhale all the odors, which will hopefully seduce the inner child. Go see the kids at the pony park, watch their enjoyment as they ride around in circles, and try to get some vicarious impact from it. Watch all the Disney movies that you watched as a child: *Snow White, Fantasia,* and all the other animated adventures that were meaningful to your inner child.

FINDING MEANINGFUL OBJECTS FROM YOUR CHILDHOOD

Look for photo albums that contain pictures of you and your family and friends. Study them, and try to go back to those times. Remember the events surrounding the pictures and sensorially re-create elements such as the weather, the sounds and odors of that place, the voices of the people in the pictures, and how you felt at that time in your life. Take a trip with each photo.

Find other objects that you collected as a child or clothes that you kept. Take out your Boy or Girl Scout uniform way back in the closet, and allow yourself to remember the events of scouting, such as hiking or cooking over a fire that you built. Always involve all of your senses when working to remember an event. I used to keep all my collected treasures in a cigar box under my bed. I had rings, belt buckles, election pins, a Boy Scout pocket knife, various buttons I had collected from clothing my mother gave to charity, a miniature camera that never worked, and a host of other memorabilia. If you too can find objects from your childhood, use them and work with them. They are rich in memories.

REACHING THE INNER CHILD
THROUGH THE UNCONSCIOUS

If, just before you fall asleep, you think about and remember many things from your early life and continue to muse about them until you fall asleep, quite often you will have dreams related to those earlier years. By doing so you are making a very important connection with your unconscious. With repetition the unconscious will release more and more inner-child experiences into your conscious behavior. The connections will manifest themselves in your improved willingness to believe. Dream work is incredible on many levels. Your dream life is extremely valuable in informing you of issues you are not really conscious of. Besides making an unconscious connection to the inner child, your dreams will contain images and experiences that you may have long forgotten.

THE ORIGINAL BEING EXERCISE

Yet another approach to the inner child, this particular exercise has many uses and goals. It is also instrumental in accessing a relationship to unconscious impulses related to the very young child that we harbor inside us. In this framework you start the exercise by simply lying down on your bed, the floor, or anywhere that is somewhat comfortable. Clear your mind of random thoughts; try to erase the noise of thinking and fleeting thoughts. After a few minutes, maybe as many as ten or fifteen, slowly open your eyes and look at what you see as if for the first time. Everything you see, feel, smell, or detect with any of your five senses should be as if for the first time. The way your fingers work and move should be a curiosity; the objects that surround you must be seen as if for the first time. Understanding them is impossible. Using your muscles or moving your arms is a discovery and an accomplishment at the same time. Sounds are confusing and need to be listened to, and finding the way your ears work is an additional discovery. Attempting to move or sit up must become a learned activity. Everything you see hasn't got a name or any association. Shapes and colors are examined and related to without any reference to prior knowledge. Explore everything; take nothing for granted. Besides being a wonderful exercise for getting selflessly involved and preparing to act, this has the power to elicit primordial impulses.

Imagine a fetus in the womb: what does it feel? At birth what are a baby's first impressions of being in the world? What does it see? feel? hear? understand?

I'M FIVE YEARS OLD AND I...

I've already described this exercise earlier in the book. It is used for a variety of purposes. It is a wonderful way to get involved and a great choice hunt for the discovery of choices that you can use in the future. In this framework the purpose is to access the inner child. Here again the actor can do the exercise in a class in front of other students or alone.

Example:

"I'm five years old and...I am playing with my little red car. Zoom, zoom, I'm turning corners. I'm five years old and...I hear my mommy in the kitchen. I smell the food cooking...it makes me feel warm...I'm five years old and I...am in my pajamas with the blue and pink animals all over them. I'm five years old, and my mommy puts me to bed, and she turns off the clown lamp. I see the shadows of the trees dancing on the ceiling. I'm in kindergarten. I play with clay and make funny things, monsters. I am painting with my fingers and it's yucky. I'm five years old, and I have a sister, and she cries all the time. I have a blue bike with training wheels, and I can ride it fine. I sit in the back of the car in a car seat. I don't like it! I'm six years old, and I started first grade. I don't like the teacher. She is old and mean. I'm six years old and my mommy takes me to school. I want to walk to school, but she won't let me. My dad is never around. He is always working, but he took me to the park last Sunday. We had fun. I love him. I'm six years old, and my friend Tommy lives next door, and we play in his backyard. He has a dog and we wrestle with him. His name is Spider. I'm six years old, and we go trick-or-treating on Halloween. I'm a pirate, and I have a sword and a patch over one of my eyes."

After exhausting five, the actor would go to six and then seven and eight and so on, emphasizing the early years. The value of this approach is in the results it produces. With daily repetition, using a variety of the suggested exercises, the actor will create a connection to the inner child, which will make all of the hypothetical elements of material believable.

I'M JUST A LITTLE BOY/GIRL AND I...

I have already described this exercise, which I do in my classes quite often for the actors to elevate their vulnerability. In this case, however, it is used to stimulate the child energy and is best done in a group, because it requires a response from the other students. The actor starts the exercise facing the people in the audience and asks a direct question to each person on a one-to-one basis, making eye contact and waiting for a response.

Example:

"I'm just a little boy and I'm afraid. I'm lost and I don't know how to get home. Will you help me find my way?" He relates to one person, waiting for that one to respond, and then he moves on to the next one. Usually each student responds positively with support and encouragement. The actor goes on: "I'm just a little boy, and I need a friend. Will you be my friend?" Again he waits for a response and then continues: "I'm just a little boy and I am lost. Will you help me find where I am? I'm just a little boy and I need someone to love me. Will you love me?"

The exercise can continue for some time, with the actor expressing real feelings and personal needs. The result accomplished with this technique is totally amazing. I have seen actors revert to childhood. Not only do they get really vulnerable, but their voices even change into another register.

TWO PERSONS SHARING CHILDHOOD EXPERIENCES WITH EACH OTHER

Yet another technique for resurrecting the inner child, this is one I have done in my own classes with a great deal of success. It can be done in a class or just between two people anywhere. Both people sit and relate to each other, sharing their childhood experiences on a here-and-now basis. In other words they relate to each other experiences that happened many years ago, but they express them in the present, and they take emotional responsibility for allowing themselves to be affected by what they share.

Example:

"I'm playing with my red fire engine in the backyard. It has a siren, and I turn it on. My mom is in the kitchen and looks out the window to see if I'm all right. I go to daycare, and they have lots of toys for me to play with, and I like the other kids, and MaryAnn is pretty. I like her. I like chocolate, but my mommy doesn't let me have too much. My dad always sneaks me a Hershey bar when he comes home. I love him!"

Both people relate in a conversational manner. They do not take turns sharing.

All of the exercises in this section should be repeated and added to a daily schedule of work.

DAYDREAMING AND FANTASIZING

At first you will have to decide to do this, since you have probably not been doing it on a regular basis. Start by imagining yourself in an environment or situation where you are the center of attention, being listened to and admired by intelligent and good-looking people, who are hanging on every word you speak. Carry the fantasy into personally satisfying areas, romantic, sexual, or rewarding in any way you desire. You may fantasize about anything and anyone. Your fantasies have no boundaries or limits and don't all have to be positive or happy. They can be confrontational and indicting. The child in you can have its say with people who were insensitive and abusive while you were growing up. You may have *imaginary monologues* with all the people you are confronting. Always attempt to bring your senses into the fantasy—the sounds, the odors, what you see with your eyes, etc. Masturbatory fantasies are not only helpful in the process but also fun to do. We look forward to that activity. Create any fantasy you want, but do it on a daily basis.

Episodic Fantasies

I have already shared with you that when I was young and hated to go to bed, I created adventures that were ongoing, often for weeks at a time. I am repeating it here purposely. One of my favorite fantasies was going through the jungles of the Dark Continent searching for the treasures of King Solomon. I knew there were incredible riches there, but I had to find the mine. I was fastidious in my preparations and my outfits. I carried food and water and hired natives to carry my supplies. We trekked for miles in mosquito-infested jungles and rivers with snakes and alligators. My journey, as I faced hungry lions and other predators, made me sweat with fear and resolve. I battled headhunters and hostile tribes that chased me and shot deadly darts dipped in poison. I always escaped after having killed many of my pursuers. Each night before I fell off to sleep I encountered an emotionally exciting adventure, which continued where I had left off the previous night. Quite often I entertained the same fantasy for months and finally discovered the mine, which led to the next fantasy of getting the treasure out of the country and going on a whirlwind adventure, as I spent the fortune all over the globe, gambling millions in Monte Carlo and sailing my yacht around the world, encountering really horrendous ocean experiences.

One of my favorite fantasies was being a gunfighter in the old West. I was the fastest gun in the West and probably in the world. They came from everywhere to challenge me, and I would honestly try to talk them out of fighting me, but most often I failed and had to shoot them down before their gun cleared the holster. I always paid for their funeral though! I spent months time traveling. Each night I would go back in time and visit another period in history. It was a great adventure, particularly since I knew what was coming. I would tell the people what to expect, but quite often they would not believe me. One of my experiences took place before the Japanese attacked Pearl Harbor. I went to the FBI, who arrested me. I had a difficult time getting out of that one. In one of my ongoing fantasies I was a clairvoyant and went around the world helping everyone to avoid oncoming disasters. Those fantasies were very impacting. I really believed in them and would sensorially experience the full impact of the times, places, people, sounds and odors of every place I visited.

The inner, magical child truly impels the actor to imagine, experience, and delight in all of the wonderful and exciting emotional arenas that he must visit.

FACILITATIONS, HABITS, AND TRAPS ACTORS FALL INTO

In this next section I will be listing many of the traps an actor can fall into and habits he can acquire that are inhibitors to organic work. If they are not dealt with or alleviated, they last a lifetime.

The tragedy is that, because of those issues, a potentially talented and creative person may never realize the depth of his or her real talent.

Over a period of time every actor finds ways to be comfortable on stage or in front of the camera. Unfortunately, without specific training and the development of a solid craft, he develops techniques and habits that do not originate from a being state or any real organic feeling. He learns to use them to approach and hopefully fulfill his obligations. I will address all of those facilitations and suggest many antidotes to each of those unfortunate indulgences. If you, the actor, recognize and identify some of those habits and traps, then you can begin a creative journey to eliminating them and becoming an authentic artist.

DEPENDENCIES

There is a long list of dependencies an actor can acquire over a period of time. All of them are obstacles to authentic and organic reality. The problem with dependencies is that they block most of the organic impulses from expression. The reason an actor holds on to them is that at one time he may have received praise for his work, and what had then been an organic response has become a behavioral dependency, which takes the place of his real impulses. Quite often dependencies are interpreted as personality traits rather than as what they really are.

VOCAL DEPENDENCY

This dependency is quite common. It is often referred to as an actor being vocally centered. The voice is like a musical instrument, which, when organically connected to an actor's feelings and emotions, can colorfully express them all, from the most obvious to the most subtle. But an actor can manipulate his voice to communicate the feelings he is attempting to express. When he intellectually colors his voice with the desired emotional expression, he creates a split, called a ***vocal-and-emotional split,*** between his real emotions and their vocal expression (I will explain splits later on). A great number of actors are vocally centered, many of them British Shakespearean actors—which is not unexplainable, since so much of the British actors' training and emphasis is on language and words. On the other end of that scale, many American actors are inarticulate and do not enunciate, even when they are organically connected to their voice.

So what is the antidote to such a dependency? How does the actor address and eliminate the problem? Well, it is not an easy task. Most dependencies are formed over a long period of time and become solidly rooted habits. Habits are hard to break and to get rid of, but not impossible. Of course, so many bad habits and dependencies result from a lack of training, from failing to acquire specific instrumental techniques as well as a solid craft. However, there are exercises that can antidote vocal dependencies once the actor is aware of the issue and willing to confront it. The first step is for him to get in touch with what he is really feeling, which is done through several exercises.

PERSONAL INVENTORY

As explained earlier, to do this exercise the actor repeatedly asks himself, *How do I feel?* and then responds with how he feels in the moment. When he is really aware of his moment-to-moment impulses and is expressing them, he should go to the lines of the material he is working on and say them *irreverently,* connecting his feelings to the lines. At that point the words should be coming from an organic source, as the actor experiences what it feels like to be connected emotionally to them. The first taste of that connection is very important in the elevation of his consciousness.

At this point the reader must be asking, What about fulfilling the author's intentions? What about the responsibilities to the material? Good questions! If the actor then works for a choice that will take him to the emotional obligation of the material, while continuing to be vocally and emotionally connected, then he is experiencing his organic truth. His performance will come from a real place, and there will be no split between what he really feels and what he is expressing.

PERSONAL INVENTORY II

This exercise was explained in the section on social blocks and obstacles. The questions *Am I expressing how I feel? and if not, why not? and what can I do to express how I feel right now?* may have to be repeated a number of times before the actor can actually express his real impulses; however, it is a way for him to discover what is blocking him and to encourage himself to express his real feelings.

NONVERBAL WORKOUTS

One of the reasons for doing nonverbal work is to eliminate logic and the connection with the meaning of words. If the actor removes the words and the emotions they suggest, he can then encourage vocal expression that comes from an organic source.

Nonverbal Imaginary Monologues

The actor can do this exercise alone or in a classroom venue. He decides to talk to people he has some emotional agenda with; he places them in empty seats and then, going from one imaginary person to another, begins to relate to each one just through sounds. The sounds will vary depending on the content of the monologue, and, from a *real* place, they will carry the emotional impulses through the voice. At that point the actor might address a written monologue he has been working on, also approaching it nonverbally. With repetition he will slowly begin to allow his impulses to affect his voice and subsequently will carry them into the written lines of a monologue or scene.

One-Sound Exercise

This is yet another technique for addressing vocal dependency. The actor makes a neutral sound and holds it for a long time, only interrupting it to take a breath. He then encourages himself to allow everything he feels from one moment to the next to affect the sound. If he allows everything that emotionally comes up, the sound will vary, and the voice will begin to have many colors and much variety. He can also express his moment-to-moment impulses to another person in the framework of the single sound. This technique will help him become conscious of the connection between what he feels and the varied expressions of those impulses through the voice.

"I FEEL..." THEN SAY THE LINE

Another good exercise to address verbal dependency is for the actor to ask herself how she feels and then respond with that impulse in the next line of her monologue. She would do this on every line as an exercise to learn to carry all of her moment-to-moment responses into the lines. It is an irreverent approach but a valuable one in the training process. This exercise can also be used as one of the anticoncept techniques, which I will address later.

IRREVERENT COMMUNICATION

Here the actor chooses to communicate either with another person or in a classroom situation through the words of a written monologue, attempting to make herself understood by expressing her feelings and impulses through the lines of the piece. This can also be done using gibberish. If the actor feels a large number of things in relation to the person or persons she is relating to, her voice will carry her emotions, and that will act as an antidote to verbal dependency.

Of course all the exercises detailed here must be repeated many times in order for them to have a lasting impact.

PHYSICAL DEPENDENCIES

These include a plethora of physical actions, *isms,* shticks, and so on, which are often created over a long period of time and which become quite unconscious. Good-looking actors get into their attractiveness and model their faces and bodies to the greatest advantage. Some of them have been known to instruct the director of photography as to which is their best side, how to best light and photograph them, or what kind of lenses to use to best capture their beauty. With preoccupations like those they would have to have been more concentrated on the physical aspects rather than the obligations to the material.

There is a long list of actors, many of them quite talented, who have developed physical dependencies. David Janssen had a number of physical mannerisms that he used to communicate emotion. He would clench his teeth, so that the muscles in his jaw would tighten and loosen when he was expressing a strong emotion. Clint Eastwood, who has made an incredible contribution to the film industry, clenches his teeth and wrinkles his lips every time he says, "Go ahead! Make my day!" Gilbert Roland, an actor from the '50s and '60s, always had his sleeves rolled up, wore a leather strap on his wrist, and was very physical in everything he acted in, always macho in every character he played.

So many actors have physical mannerisms, which become traits people attribute to their personality, but which are in reality repeated actions that do not for the most part come from real organic impulses and in fact probably get in the way of their connection to the impulses that are taking place in the moment. One might ask, So what? I enjoy watching those actors. I might say that too, but the real issue is that there is a disconnection from the flow of organic moment-to-moment impulses, and once the flow is disrupted, it short-circuits all of the impulses that follow and could be expressed, much as when a freight train comes to a quick stop and all the cars crash into each other.

So how can an actor correct and eliminate physical dependencies? That is difficult to do, because so much of an actor's process is dependent on his being able to come from a being place. If the actor is trained to be in the moment and to use a process that addresses the obligations of the material, and if he includes all of his moment-to-moment impulses, so that he is totally connected to what is going on in the moment and allows himself to express and discover the next moment in the next moment, then he will not be prone to developing physical dependencies or repeatedly expressing them. So many of the obstacles detailed in this book relate to the actor's training and his connection with his authenticity.

Another way for you to address this issue is to become aware of the dependencies, to watch and spot them daily when they happen, and to make adjustments while working to become more organically involved in the impetus that creates your behavior in a scene. Consciousness and awareness can go a long way in eliminating a large portion of those dependencies.

BEHAVIORAL DEPENDENCIES

Many of the categories of dependency cross over into each other. A behavioral dependency is not necessarily emotional or vocal, but it can manifest itself physically. Rod Steiger, a very talented actor, who comes from the same orientation as my background includes, was full of shticks and *isms* and also included many vocal dependencies in his work. When he played Al Capone, he spent many minutes eating an apple while on the telephone with someone. All one could watch was the way he ate that apple. It was quite a shtick! Burt Lancaster had many emotional dependencies and in his early years was also a very physical actor. In *Elmer Gantry* and *The Rainmaker* he was essentially over the top and theatrical. While they were interesting and charismatic, his actions were also manifestations of behavioral dependencies. Although in many cases those dependencies are compelling to watch, they are **impositional** expressions nonetheless. What does that mean? It means that the behavior comes from a premeditated or structured place rather than from organic reality. For example, if an actor is very animated and, like Lancaster, is somewhat over the top, that behavior should come from an organic impetus. If he has a craft, a process for creating reality, the choices he uses will stimulate the kind of behavior that is obligated by the material.

Many actors are behaviorally dependent. The proof of that is in their repetition of the same expression in everything they do. Jeff Goldblum, who is also a good actor, has behavioral mannerisms that appear in everything he does. In the middle of a line he will stutter a little, stop, look as if he were mentally searching for something, and then continue to speak. If he did that once in a while, it would seem to come from a real place. It is, however, present in everything he does and may have its source in a number of areas. It may be the result of his attempt to be natural and real, and possibly at one time it did come from a real impulse; but since it worked once, twice, or three times, it became a behavioral mannerism. He is interesting to watch, but wouldn't he be even more effective if those moments were filled with the real impulses that hide under the dependency? Jack Nicholson, who I think is one of the best actors in the world and is a longtime friend of mine, has some interesting behavioral manifestations, which are endearing as well. They go back forty years or so. Even when we were in acting class together Jack expressed himself that way. He would tip his head back a little and look at you as if he knew something about you that you didn't know he knew, and a slight smile would cross his face; or that same look would register as if he had a secret joke on the world and was the only person who knew the joke. It would make the other actor extremely uncomfortable, as it always made me feel.

Then there is Meryl Streep, who loves doing a large variety of accents, which seem to serve as hooks for her to hang her character on. She even played an old Jewish man, a rabbi, replete with not too authentic a Jewish accent. She appears to use the accents as a behavioral dependency, a springboard to help her construct the character she plays. I even heard her say on an interview that she has no process and that she simply reads and rereads the scripts until she gets a "feeling" about the character.

EMOTIONAL DEPENDENCIES

There are the criers, the laughers, the raging ones, the contemplators, and the phumpernicks (actors who make "phumph" sounds in between their lines). You see them repeating their emotional shticks almost every time they are on the stage or in a film. We even become accustomed to expecting their antics when we watch them. Those dependencies are usually the result of an originally successful acting experience and become dependencies because they work. They are repeated because they communicate an emotional state that the actor feels addresses the requirements of the scene. There was an actor whose name was Max Showalter. In everything I ever saw him in he would laugh, sometimes even when it was inappropriate. It was obviously a redirection of what he was experiencing. I'm not sure that he had any awareness of it. His laugh was quite pleasant and could sometimes be interpreted as good-natured, but it rarely came from a real place. Another great laugher, someone I toured in a play with, was Robert Middleton. He worked in a large number of films and would laugh infectiously somewhere in every role. It was definitely an emotional dependency. In the '40s Bobs Watson, a child actor who was about nine or ten years old, could cry on cue, and his tears could break your heart. He was always hired to do just that. Al Pacino, who happens to be one of my favorite actors, will also from time to time explode, full of rage, to highlight a moment. I think those outbursts are premeditated and become an occasional dependency. Marlon Brando was full of emotional dependencies, quite often understated with predictable mannerisms. We have all seen actors raging on stage, whose rage was somehow unsupported by real impulses.

I have used the few examples above to describe the dependencies created by actors. You must begin to become aware of your own dependencies in all areas and to address them, so that ultimately you may get rid of them by replacing them with a connection to your real impulses. At the root of many of those dependencies is tension. Many actors either redirect their tension into behavior or they will use it as a manifestation of the required emotion. In either case the real emotion and impulses are buried beneath the tension or the redirected behavior. Tension is the manifestation of unexpressed impulses that are conglomerated into a ball of energy, which, when used as an organic response, does not really represent the truth of the obligated emotional state. I have coined a phrase describing this phenomenon: "theatrical hysteria," more commonly known as "ass energy." Many famous actors have created careers using their tension to fuel their performances. Jack Palance created and worked off his tension energy for many years. In his later work—I suppose because he became more secure—he started to function more organically and, as a result, was more interesting to watch.

INTELLECTUAL DEPENDENCIES

This area of dependency is extremely common. It usually manifests in actors who are easily intimidated by emotion, have difficulty stimulating strong emotions, or have grown up in an emotionally conservative environment. It can also be the result of reaching comfort by appearing simple and controlled. Whatever the case may be, it is a phenomenon that I have called *mind-mouth connection.* John Houseman was very intellectually dependent in his work. I don't think I ever heard him raise his voice or express any kind of theatrical emotion. Patrick Stewart is not only intellectually dependent, but also vocally centered and dependent. Lloyd Bochner, who worked a lot in the eighties, I believe was also vocally and intellectually dependent. I name those people to give the reader some evidence of how the various dependencies manifest themselves, and not as a criticism of the actors I use as examples. Everyone does the best he can, and criticism is an odious and unfair thing for one artist to level against another.

This type of dependency short-circuits the connection between the stimulus and an organic emotional response. Instead of responding the way he is affected by what is happening in the scene, the actor sends all of his impulses into his head and then manipulates his behavior into the words, creating an *intellectual-and-emotional split.* In addition, he may choreograph his voice to carry his conceptual emotions, creating a second split, a *vocal-and-emotional* one. Actors who function that way are usually very articulate and, unfortunately, predictable. Classically trained actors are prone to becoming very intellectually oriented as well as dependent on their voice and words. Laurence Olivier, for example, would write notes on a script to choreograph the volume and intonation of his voice in certain sections and lines. It is very difficult to serve Shakespeare's meter without falling into vocal and intellectual traps, although some classical actors have found ways to address the material and still be connected to their impulses and emotions.

ELIMINATING THE DEPENDENCIES

Addressing those dependencies is quite complicated because it has so many variables. If an actor is instrumentally open, free of blocks and obstacles, and he has a very solid craft, then he can deal with those dependencies successfully. Unfortunately, most actors are not instrumentally free to act, and even if they think they have a process, it has been my experience over the years to learn that they really do not!

The reason those dependencies and splits exist is that the actor's concentration goes to the wrong places. If he is involved in working for an affecting choice, is functioning on a moment-to-moment basis, and is being affected by his choice, he cannot service a conceptual idea or behave separately from the reality in the moment. When his concentration goes to servicing the moment from any other place than his reality, that is when the conceptual behavior and the dependencies take over. So what is the answer? How does an actor who has been acting for decades address those splits? Well, even if it is incredibly difficult to accept, he must think about retraining his instrument and learning a specific process that will antidote all of the problems he has. I understand that this is a very tall order, which would probably be resisted by almost every actor reading this; however, short of going back to square one, I will attempt to suggest some exercises that will help to eliminate many of the dependencies, as well as to focus the actor in a more creative direction.

A MOMENT-TO-MOMENT RUNNING INNER MONOLOGUE

I have already suggested that the actor use both Personal Inventories to get in touch with what he is really feeling, expressing it through the lines. If he starts to become aware and creates a running inner monologue before and after saying the lines of the scene, also running it in between the lines and under them, this technique will focus him on what he is experiencing in the moment. If, in addition, he is responding to available stimuli and a choice that is affecting him, his involvement and focus will shift from listening to himself and leading his behavior in a cerebral and conceptual manner.

Example:

The actor begins to formulate the inner monologue in words, running it under the lines of the scene: *I feel aware of what I am doing. It feels strange, but I am feeling impulses that are not what I think I should be feeling. I am being affected by the way she is looking at me, and it embarrasses me a little. I wonder if I am turning red. I feel a little flushed. I am attracted to her and I am supposed to be, so I guess I should let that happen. I feel strange and yet I feel good. I am saying the words of the scene, and they feel different to me. I am not listening to myself. I am more involved with her, and that feels good too.*

While that is going on, the actor should include all of those feelings and impulses into the lines and his expression. If he does just this much, he will avoid leading himself into imposing behavior that is not authentic.

BEING IRREVERENT TO YOUR CONCEPT OF THE MATERIAL

There are two ways to approach this exercise: In a rehearsal of the monologue or scene that you are doing, say the lines while being totally irreverent to the obligations of the material, allowing yourself to go moment to moment with your impulses and feelings, and expressing everything that comes up on a moment-to-moment basis. Approaching the dependency in this manner frees you from any responsibility to fulfill your emotional concept of the material. By so doing, you will hopefully avoid falling into the trap of leading yourself to address the material from an intellectually or vocally dependent place.

The second way to approach this exercise is to work for a choice that addresses the obligations of the material and the author's intentions. In that case, while your choice is designed to stimulate the emotional life required by the scene, you must include all of your impulses that may be irreverent to your concept of the behavior and express those impulses while working to fulfill the obligations. By including all of your impulses and feelings and expressing them, you will be more organic, more in the moment, and definitely unpredictable. This technique also antidotes the traps of dependency.

SPLITS

When the instrument is functioning as it should, the mind, the body, the emotions, and the voice all function normally as a unit. Nothing belies the truth of the moment. However, when the actor is not expressing her real moment-to-moment impulses, splits occur. You have all seen actors expressing strong emotions while their bodies seem totally disconnected from what they are expressing. Their arms and legs appear fixed in a position that doesn't seem to go along with their emotional expression. That constitutes a physical-and-emotional split. The reason it happens is that the actor disconnects from her real impulses and imposes an emotional state over what she is really feeling.

There are several obvious splits that take place when the actor is disconnected from her reality. Vocal-and-emotional splits are quite common. I already explained that they happen when the actor manipulates her voice to express emotions that she thinks should be there. Instead of honoring her real feelings and working for a choice to stimulate the emotional life that she obligated herself to, she short-circuits her real impulses and imposes the emotions that she feels are right for the scene, thereby creating a split between her voice and her real emotions. An intellectual split occurs when the actor is functioning from her head. She is dependent on her intellect and her concept of behavior to direct her expression. Unfortunately, when that happens, the rest of her instrument goes into a split. The words and the intonations of her voice don't seem supported by her body or her emotions, and she seems to become totally dependent on the voice and the words. Splits are always the result of a lack of connection with real impulses.

How can an actor deal with those splits? Well, since most of those issues are the result of not expressing true impulses and feelings, she must become aware of what leads her to disconnect from what is real. One of the most important exercises an actor has at her disposal is *Personal Inventory*. If she becomes aware of the splits, she can go to Personal Inventory to find out what she is really feeling and then begin to include everything she feels on a moment-to-moment basis. Once she reconnects with the flow of her real impulses and includes them in her expression, the split will totally disappear. The problem most actors encounter is that they feel that if they do that they are violating the emotional content the material demands of them. When that happens, they most often go back to imposing the proper emotional expression, which causes them to create a split again. There are two- and three-way splits and even four-way splits. A split is the instrument's lie detector.

COMPENSATIONAL BEHAVIOR

This is a very common trap for many actors. Actually, it is a way for them to impose a more acceptable emotional response or expression when what they are really feeling is uncomfortable or exposing in an unacceptable way. For example, if the actor feels very tense, in an effort to hide that tension he *compensates* by imposing a relaxed physical demeanor and in addition modulates his voice to cover the tension he is experiencing. He might also compensate when he has an uncomfortable impulse, an emotion he has avoided feeling or dealing with in his life. Most people hide their embarrassment, so when an actor feels embarrassed on the stage, his immediate impulse is to redirect and compensate by imposing another more acceptable emotion. In doing so, however, he short-circuits the connection with what he is really feeling and thereby behaves from a place that does not really have an organic source.

Conceptual compensation occurs when the actor feels that he is not addressing his concept of the material (I will describe and define concept later in this section). Let us imagine that he is experiencing a response to his choice and that he is connected to that emotional life but feels that it violates his concept of the character's behavior. At that point he will redirect his organic impulse by compensating and imposing another emotion.

There are physical, intellectual, and psychological compensations. For example, if an actor feels physically awkward in a scene, he might adjust his body so as to appear less so. There are many ways he may compensate physically. While playing a romantic scene, for example, he might feel less attractive than he imagines he should be, so he might compensate by assuming a more masculine persona. Quite often it is very obvious when he is split. An *intellectual compensation* occurs when the actor feels that his behavior and his emotional expression are not in sync with how he has interpreted the character's behavior in the scene or moment. He will make a behavioral adjustment to satisfy his intellectual interpretation. *Psychological compensations* are similar to intellectual compensations. The actor will adjust his expression to match his psychological interpretation of where the character is in the scene.

It is only when an actor is functioning from his real emotional base that he is expressing his true impulses and is being an **experiential actor**. In every compensational involvement the actor is disconnected from his organic impulses and is behaving in an assumed way. What he may really be feeling is separate from what he is expressing, and his behavior becomes representational rather than real. All of that is a result of not being involved with a choice, an impetus that will affect him in the emotional areas of the obligations of the material. Here is where having a specific craft is so important. If the actor is really involved in the stimulus and is impelled to behave as a result of the way he is affected by it, he will be honestly connected to what he is feeling on an organic moment-to-moment basis.

A number of exercises and techniques are helpful in addressing the problem. They all start with getting selflessly involved. If the actor can get involved with anything outside himself, that is the first step in antidoting compensational behavior. Whatever the obligations of the scene are, he must first get out of his own way by getting involved with the other actor or the environment. An excellent exercise is Observe, Perceive, and Wonder.

OBSERVE, PERCEIVE, AND WONDER

This exercise can be done as a preparation for getting ready to approach a scene and is almost always successful in liberating the actor from his self-involvement. It can be done out loud, or silently as an inner monologue.

The actor can observe, perceive, and wonder in relation to anything—the people, the environment, or the specific objects in a room. When getting involved with another actor he is about to work with, he can focus on that person. Observation is simply relating to the things that are there. Perception is a much deeper form of observation, where, for example, you look deeply into a person's eyes to perceive her feelings or the emotion that is there; you observe the expressions, interpret what they mean, perceive the body language and what that tells you, listen to the sounds in the person's voice and what they are communicating, and so on. Wondering simply means that you wonder about the person in any area that occurs to you, elevating your curiosity to the tenth level.

Example:

(*Relating to the other actor.*) "I see that you are dressed rather neatly and that you are color coordinated. I perceive that you pay a lot of attention to the way you look, and there might also be some concern about how other people see you. I wonder if that is true." (The other actor may or may not answer or respond. It is very important that the actor doing the exercise not relate anything back to himself, since that would not encourage selfless involvement.) "I see that you are a little embarrassed by what I am saying. I wonder why. I perceive that you are shy and observe that you are folding your arms across your midsection. I think that is a way you hide or protect yourself. I wonder how old you are, and I know that you will not answer that, and that's OK. I see that you look away frequently, avoiding eye contact with me. Are you aware of that? I perceive that I am putting you on the spot and am making you uncomfortable, and that is not my purpose at all. I see that your foot is moving in small circles and that you are tense across your shoulders also. I wonder what would happen if you did with me what I am doing with you. I think it would get you out of yourself. You smiled. You have a beautiful smile and, wow, what great teeth! You look so clean and put together. I wonder how often you go to the hairdresser. I wonder what kind of perfume you wear. I perceive that you are somewhat more comfortable. I wonder if it's because you feel more accepted now."

The exercise can go on for as long as it needs to in order to get the actor selflessly involved.

It is important to note here that all of the exercises suggested in relation to compensation are designed so that the actor can get out of himself. The obstacle or issue that separates him from involvement with the stimulus, the choice that is selected to address the author's intent, is most often his involvement with himself, his self-consciousness, or his awareness of what the expectations are. Getting selflessly involved is the first step towards using a choice to stimulate the life that is obligated by the material.

PERSONAL POINT OF VIEW

This is another good technique for eliminating self-involvement and all the ills that come from it. Refer to the section on emotional insecurities for an example of the exercise. It can go on for as long as it is necessary for the actor to get totally out of himself. Selfless involvement doesn't mean that you are ready to act; it simply liberates you from having your eyes turned inward on yourself. If you are free of internal comments, you are not prone to compensating in any area.

THE ENSEMBLE EXERCISE

This too is a good selfless-involvement technique, and it is also effective for getting involved with the other actor. Two actors sit or stand, facing each other, and relate by using the approach. One of them starts by saying, "You make me feel good being with you."

The other actor responds to that statement with how it made her feel: "I like what you said, and now I feel more comfortable with you."

He responds, "Now I feel free to tell you that I am attracted to you."

She says, "That makes me feel a little nervous, and I don't know how to respond to that."

He retorts, "That makes me feel like you think I'm coming on to you, and I'm not."

She responds, "Now I feel a little better and less obligated to say or do something."

He remarks, "Now I feel a little rejected and misunderstood!"

She says, "That makes me angry. Why is it that there is always an underlying sexual issue between men and women? Why can't the gender issue just be an issue of two people?"

He may take a moment before responding, "Now I feel chastised by you. What in the hell is wrong with someone admiring another person of the opposite sex?"

She replies, "Well, I'm sorry that you are angry, but if you were a woman you would understand how often men come on to us."

He is affected by her last statement and takes a moment to respond, "I do understand, even if I'm not a woman, but you should be able to tell the difference between a come-on and a compliment."

She responds, "That makes me feel like I jumped to conclusions about what you said, and I'm sorry."

He says, "OK, I accept your apology, and now I feel we can start to relate on a new level."

She says, "Now I feel much better and even closer to you."

This exercise, not only liberates the actors from being self-involved, but is also a great approach for them when they want to stimulate a creative dependency on each other, and it is a wonderful way of creating **ensemble.** By responding on a moment-to-moment basis to the way each of them is affected by what is said, they establish a complete creative dependency on each other, and the level of involvement and unpredictability is extremely high.

The structure of the exercise is:

"You make me feel..."

"That makes me feel..."

"Now I feel..."

The actors respond to each of those statements with how they are affected in the moment.

MOMENT-TO-MOMENT INCLUSIONS

Another very good technique for getting the actor out of himself, as well as establishing an organic moment-to-moment flow of impulses, is to include and express all the feelings and impulses that come up in the moment. This can be done as a stream of consciousness or in the framework of saying the lines in a scene or monologue. If it is done as a stream of consciousness, the actor simply expresses whatever comes up in the moment—a point of view, a response to the environment, a distraction, a comment, or anything else. By including what is really going on moment to moment, he is freed from the kind of commentary that leads to adjusting his behavior in a compensatory way. If he is doing a scene or a monologue, it might sound like the example below.

Example:

(Using the monologue in the scene from *The Glass Menagerie* where Tom speaks to his mother, Amanda.)

"Do you think I am crazy about the *warehouse?*...Sure, every time you come in yelling that bloody *Rise and Shine!* Rise and Shine!! I think how lucky dead people are!" (At this point the actor feels uncomfortable and allows himself to include that impulse, either internally as an inner monologue or, if he is in rehearsal, audibly.) *I feel disconnected. I have to reinvest in my choice. I'm using her, so I have to involve myself in the negative aspect of the choice.* (All of this is included in his behavior as he continues to say the words of the monologue.) "But I get up. I *go!* For sixty-five dollars a month I give up all that I dream of..." (Again he feels an impulse coming up for him that could be distracting if not included.) *Yeah, that's right, I do give up a lot to be an actor!* "If self is all I ever thought of, Mother, *I'd* be where *he* is." (Pointing at his father's picture.) *Wow, where did they get that ugly guy?*

All of those moment-to-moment comments and impulses must be included in the behavior of the actor. If they are parenthesized, they will short-circuit the connection with his organic impulses and create a split.

All of those exercises are designed to liberate the actor from his self-involvement and what it leads to; but without a craft or process to go to, he cannot address or fulfill the obligations of the material. One suggestion I have for any actor is to use *Available Stimulus.* It is a simple choice approach that can be used to address the responsibilities of the material.

USING AVAILABLE STIMULUS

After the actor successfully becomes selflessly involved, he must be able to go to the obligations of the scene, one of which is what he is feeling emotionally or in relation to the other actor. If he has no process, creating that reality would be difficult. So I am suggesting a simple choice approach that will work at least to fulfill the relationship obligation.

If the actor knows what the material demands, he can use the other actor to stimulate the desired emotional state. For example, if he is supposed to be attracted to her, then he could **selectively**

emphasize the attractive things about her exclusively. By relating only to those things, he will begin to have all of the feelings that the material demands. If, on the other hand, he must feel very negative feelings in relation to her, he could do the opposite, looking for and emphasizing all of the negative physical features and behaviors he is experiencing from her. He might see some criticism in her eyes or detect some judgment in her voice; he might interpret her body language as rejecting or protective, and so on. Using Available Stimulus is easy and almost always works to stimulate the desired response.

REDIRECTION

This is yet another obstacle an actor can create that gets in the way of his organic connection with the material. When the actor experiences an impulse which is uncomfortable or does not service what he believes should be there, he will redirect the authentic impulse into a more acceptable emotional response or expression. By doing that, he creates a split between what he is really experiencing and what is being expressed, and he thereby short-circuits the efficacy of his reality. It is very similar to compensation, except for the fact that a compensation can be changing one moment of an emotional state whereas redirection is often an entire intellectual, physical, and emotional alteration in behavior. In many cases it is an instrumental issue: if the actor is inhibited in certain emotional areas and is affected in a way that stimulates an emotional response he is afraid of or uncomfortable with, he will substitute the real impulse with one he feels more comfortable with. Unfortunately, this creates a split that is difficult to repair and that prevents him from getting back to an organic state. If the actor has sufficient tools, a craft that will allow him to *re-invest* in his choice, however, he can overcome the result of the redirection.

Sometimes the actor will redirect an impulse because what he may be experiencing violates his connection with the concept he has about the scene. If he redirects because he has a strong concept about what the character is feeling or expressing, then once again he is probably functioning from a cerebral place and is not connected to his real organic feelings. In any case redirection splits the actor, who can then only premeditate and impose expression. Many of the traps an actor can fall into often overlap each other. In almost every instance it comes down to the fact that he is not functioning from a real place. If he redirects because he is inhibited in certain emotional and expressive areas, he needs to deal with and eliminate the blocks that he has conditioned. Earlier in this book I listed a large number of exercises in a variety of instrumental areas that address many of those problems. If indeed the behavior is a result of an inhibition in a certain area, the actor must specifically define the block and find exercises that are designed to alleviate it. The first step is to become aware that he is in fact redirecting his real impulses into other expressions. If he can accomplish that, then he can do an *inner monologue* coupled with *Personal Inventory,* which will allow him to get back to his real impulses and feelings.

INNER MONOLOGUE WITH PERSONAL INVENTORY

An inner monologue is done by simply speaking internally. It is not an intellectual process and is quite different from thinking. You just form the words internally. It is also a choice approach in my system and is used in many areas and with many choices. When the actor becomes aware of the split and of the fact that he is redirecting what he is really feeling, he starts the inner monologue, asking himself, *How am I feeling?* He responds to what he discovers and includes those impulses in his expression. Once he connects to what is going on emotionally, he expresses those impulses as part of the scene or monologue that he is doing. The inclusion becomes part of what the character is experiencing and causes the actor's behavior to be more unpredictable and colorful. What keeps most actors from including what they feel in any given moment is the fear that they will be distorting the emotional meaning of the piece. That is a totally false concept.

Once the actor has alleviated the redirection, he must then reinvest in his choice, or whatever he is working on, to get back to the obligation of the material. If the actor has a craft, he will have no problem getting back on track.

IMPOSITION

This occurs when the actor imposes a behavior or emotional expression that she feels should be there in the scene or in that particular moment. It does not come from a real place and is usually contrived. Unfortunately, many actors who impose an emotion or a response become quite facile at making it look real, and consequently they get away with it. Many fairly successful actors are presentational. Even though they have earned respect in the field, their work lacks depth and unpredictability. Some of them have a charismatic personality, so the audience finds them attractive and is willing to identify with them, but the reality is that they are consummate fakers.

So what can someone who is prone to imposition do about it? Well, it is not that simple! The actor must first acknowledge that she is imposing and that she is not connected to her real impulses and feelings while she is acting. If indeed she is willing to address the problem, she can begin using many of the exercises already mentioned throughout this book. It is an arduous journey breaking a habit that has persisted for many years. I have always told actors that they should not try to break the habit but to replace it with a better one. When the dust settles, it really comes down to the fact that the actor must decide what kind of actor she wants to be.

CONCEPT

This is probably the most common of all the issues an actor has to deal with. It simply means that from the outset he gets an idea of what the play and the character are about, and from that point on he begins to conceptualize all of his behavior and relationships. All of his emotions are assumed or imposed, and his performance becomes an intellectual exercise that is totally supported by presentational behaviors. From the moment the actor identifies what the character and the statement of the play are, he sets forth on his journey to fulfill those original concepts, which rarely change. He proceeds to assume and impose behaviors and emotions that come from his head. The emotional life is presentational and lacks any connection with organic reality.

I have created a number of anticoncept exercises that I have successfully used in my classes. They also address some of the other indulgences that actors are prone to, such as compensational behavior, redirection, imposition, commentary, splits, leadership, and premeditation.

INNER-OUTER MONOLOGUE

This is an excellent anticoncept exercise, which, with repetition, really helps the actor become aware of his attachment to concept. Using any monologue he knows or a section of a scene he is doing or has done, he says a few of the lines from the piece and then includes his inner impulses and feelings, going back and forth between the material and what he is personally feeling on a moment-to-moment basis.

Example:

(For this example I will be using Tom's monologue from *The Glass Menagerie.*)

"I didn't go to the moon. I went much farther." (At this point the actor expresses exactly what he is feeling in the moment.) *I heard my voice and the way I said that line and it sounded fake to me.* (Back to the monologue.) "For time is the longest distance between two places." (Back to the expression of what he is feeling.) *I feel really disconnected from the meaning of the lines and what Tom is feeling, and I don't know how to connect with my own feelings in this moment.* (Back to the monologue.) "I...from then on, followed in my father's footsteps. The cities swept about me like dead leaves...." (Back to the actor's impulses.) *I feel a connection with what those words mean to me. I am thinking and feeling what I believe Tom is feeling. I like the connection.* "I run into a movie or a bar...." *I'm feeling that I forgot a line or two, but I feel more connected to my real impulses.* "I pass by the lighted window of a shop where perfume is sold. The window is filled with pieces of colored glass...." *I feel a little distracted at the moment and have other thoughts and feelings crashing in, and I'm a little confused.* "Then at once my sister touches my shoulder....Oh, Laura, Laura...I am more faithful than I intended to be!...For nowadays the world is lit by lightning!" *I think I forgot a whole section here, but I am affected by these lines and I feel vulnerable. Don't know why, but it's OK.* "Blow out your candles, Laura....And so, good-bye." *Wow, that was strange but interesting!*

When he is doing this exercise, the actor must include his inner expression in the next line and carry those impulses and feelings into the monologue. What that accomplishes is to liberate him from the concept. It brings his real impulses into the monologue and makes the behavior much more real, colorful, and unpredictable. Every inclusion of what he is feeling in each moment must be emotionally carried into the next line of the monologue, even if it is totally irreverent to the author's intention. Repeating the inner-outer monologue exercise will ultimately make the actor aware of the importance of including his inner impulses in the expression of the lines and will begin to liberate him from conceptual attachment.

"I FEEL..." THEN SAY THE LINE

This is another technique for liberating the actor from his intellectual and conceptual attachments. I already explained it in the section on vocal dependency. The actor continues asking himself how he feels before each line of the monologue and carries his impulses into the next line. Of course, his expressions will most likely be totally irreverent to the emotional obligations of the material, but that will certainly make him aware of the difference between imposing conceptual emotions into the lines and organically including his real moment-to-moment impulses into his expression. In order to apply this technique the actor must be aware of how he really feels from moment to moment, which is not as simple as it may sound. If, for example, he has done this piece a number of times, he may be very conceptually attached to how it is delivered. There is also the possibility that he is not habitually aware or connected to his internal impulses, which would make it very difficult for him to do this exercise. In that case he must begin by doing an in-depth **Personal Inventory** to get in touch with where he is and what he is feeling. He may have to do this repeatedly and for a long time. Once he establishes a connection with his real organic feelings, he can then attempt to do the exercise.

Example:

Using the same monologue from *The Glass Menagerie,* the actor says, *I feel,* and hopefully connects with his impulse. In this case he may feel confused, so he includes that confusion in the first line: "I didn't go to the moon. I went much farther." The line includes the expression of his confusion. Again he says, *I feel,* and this time he may feel something else, and whatever he feels must be brought into the next line: "For time is the longest distance between two places." He says, *I feel silly doing this damn exercise,* and again, his feelings are brought into the emotional expression of the next line, and so on through the entire piece.

PERSONAL POINT OF VIEW

I already gave an example of how to do this exercise in the section on emotional insecurities, so refer to it there. It can go on for five or ten minutes until the actor is totally in touch with how he feels about whatever comes up in each moment. The value of this technique is that the actor establishes a connection with his emotional point of view from one moment to the next. When that is accomplished, he may be able to include those impulses in the material he is doing. Of course, if the goal is to fulfill the obligation of the piece, he must work for choices that stimulate the emotional life required.

PROFESSOR IRWIN KORY

I described this one too earlier. It is also a great exercise for eliminating the attachment to concept. If the actor practices it and is able to give himself to the lack of logic and meaning, he will be able to generate a greater trust in his moment-to-moment impulses. One of the important values of this technique is that it establishes impulsivity and breaks the attachment to logic and meaning. If the actor can attain greater security in allowing the next moment to be unpredictable, he may then be able to carry that trust into his acting.

NONVERBAL EXERCISES

There is a large group of nonverbal workouts that are used for a variety of reasons, an important one of which is to get the actor away from the logic and meaning of the words. I already listed some of those exercises in the section on vocal dependency. Quite often words become the method of emotional communication and carry what the actor is supposedly feeling, thereby relieving him of the responsibility to express his organic emotions. In the case of concept, nonverbal work essentially forces the actor to express what he is feeling in the moment. If he understands the emotional obligations of the scene, he can then go moment to moment with his irreverent feelings or he can use a choice to address those obligations. In either case he will be liberated from the logic and meaning of the words.

In the nonverbal approach the actor uses gibberish or sounds to express what he is feeling, thereby making a connection with it, which, even if it is irreverent to the material, will wean him away from concept.

Disconnected Impulsivity

This is a hard one to describe on paper. It is, however, a magnificent exercise for creating complete impulsivity and getting out of one's head. It has three parts: In the first part, with great speed and using only sounds, the actor points to objects in the room and responds impulsively to the way they affect him. There isn't any way to describe his responses, because they are totally impulsive and seem to have no logic attached to them. After doing this for a few minutes, he will go to the second part of the exercise, which is done in gibberish. Speed is extremely important here, because, if the exercise is done properly, it does not allow the actor to get into his head. The third part is done in English. Again with great speed the actor expresses his impulses without theme or logic. It is the continuation of what he has been expressing in gibberish.

Example (in English):

(With extreme verbal speed.) "There two fronds, equal things, red color and high, hot, energy in a small room, smoke in the tunnel, movie news, Charlie Chaplin in color, energy popping in my nose, angel hair flying in formation, big, big translucent shapes haunting, a little old lady eating oranges, zip zap, smell the flowers on the grave, top hat and tails, he can't play the piano, on a skateboard in Atlantic City, hot dogs floating, the Milky Way has no milk, don't smile don't laugh, you are here and there and that's no place to be, lights, dark, gray stone on the floor, wings, fly on the wall listening, wow what in the hell is that?"

This can go on for as long as the actor wants to do it. This approach really takes him into his impulsive expression, and if he would move into the words of a monologue, being irreverent to the author's intentions, he would be able to say the lines from a completely impulsive place. With that experience he would become conscious of what going moment to moment really means.

POTPOURRI OF MONOLOGUES

Another very good training exercise to antidote concept is to use three separate monologues, going from one to the other. If the actor is coming from a real organic place and is expressing his impulses on a moment-to-moment basis, all three monologues will sound like the same piece of material—somewhat bizarre I admit, but sounding like a stream of conscious delivery of what might be a character free associating. The value of this approach is that the actor will learn to honor what he is experiencing and carry it into the lines of the separate pieces. Every exercise and technique in this section can be used to address all of the habits and traps an actor can fall into.

Example:

I will be using monologues from three plays: *I Never Sang for My Father, Death of a Salesman,* and *All My Sons.* It is important that the actor doing this exercise know that he can pick up each monologue anywhere he wants, at the beginning, the middle, or the end. It is essential that he not fall into the trap of being loyal to the concept or meaning of the words of the piece.

The actor could start the exercise with *I Never Sang for My Father:* "That night I left my father's house forever...I took the first right and the second left...and this time I went as far as California..." At this point he would go into the second monologue, *Death of a Salesman:* "I ran down eleven flights with a pen in my hand today...and suddenly I stopped, you hear?" Then he may move into the third monologue: "It takes a little time to toss that off. Because they weren't just men." Maybe he would go back to the second monologue and would pick up where he left off: "And in the middle of that office building...I saw...do you hear this!—I stopped in the middle of that building and I saw...the sky." Back to the third monologue, from *All my Sons:* "For instance, one time it'd been raining several days and this kid came to me, and gave me his last pair of dry socks. Put them in my pocket." Back to the first monologue: "Peggy and I visited him once or twice...and then he came to California to visit us, and had a fever and swollen ankles, and we put him in a hospital." Going back to the second monologue: "I saw the things that I love in this world; the work and the food and time to sit and smoke."

The actor could continue the exercise for as long as he wanted to; and again, if he was true to his real organic impulses and he allowed those impulses to come through the lines on a moment-to-moment basis, it would all sound like the ramblings of someone free associating while expressing his feelings.

The exercises listed under "Concept" are applicable to many of the other indulgences actors fall into. They all address the need for the actor to become aware that he has to solve his instrumental problems and make contact with his organic impulses. Quite often, even after acting for many years, an actor is very unaware of the blocks and issues that have created the bad habits he has acquired.

PRESENTATIONAL AND REPRESENTATIONAL ACTING

Like imposition, this is when the actor presents or represents the character and all of his behavior from an intellectual origin and adopts behavioral gestures and vocal impositions to promote his concept of the character in the piece. He may choreograph his voice to emphasize certain moments in his expression; his body language will reflect the way in which he supposes the character moves; and he will manipulate his emotions to fulfill what he intellectually believes the character would do and express. He anticipates behavior and plays the result before there is any real or organic impetus to respond. Here again the antidote is dependent on awareness and the desire to change.

PREMEDITATION

This is a very common acting problem. It occurs when the actor plans his expression and even plans how to say the lines, how they should sound when he says them. In this instance the actor is functioning almost totally from an intellectual area. As he does the scene, he is thinking ahead of what he is saying or doing. He *premeditates* his actions, his emotions, and the way he is going to behave. It is a way for him to fulfill his concept of the character's behavior. Unfortunately, there is not a shred of reality in his performance. Whatever he is really feeling is subverted and pushed down, while his impositional premeditated behavior takes over. As premeditative acting turns into a habit, it becomes the way he approaches every role. Until he becomes conscious of what he is doing and wishes to make changes, nothing will interrupt his approach to acting. I have heard actors say that they were trained to work from the outside in, when the reality is that they are working from the outside to the outside!

Almost every trap the actor falls into is the result of separating from his experiential self. What that simply means is that his real emotional life is cut off from what he is expressing in the moment. Trust plays a large part in enabling him to go to his real impulses. A great deal of his problems can be traced back to the instrumental obstacles he has. Ego, self-esteem, and a healthy sense of who you are play a large part in accomplishing a level of trust in yourself. Here again I must stress the incredible importance of instrumental liberation in every actor's training. In all of the instrumental traps an actor falls into—splits, redirection, compensational behavior, commentary, and so on—he must first acknowledge the indulgences and want to liberate himself from them. Once he becomes aware of what he is doing, he can address changing the habits by getting in touch with his real impulses. Many of the exercises that relate to premeditation are used in relation to concept also, so I detailed all of them in that section. Moment-to-Moment Inclusions is also a good way to get in touch with your real internal life and impulses.

MOMENT-TO-MOMENT INCLUSIONS

In the midst of a premeditated expression the actor can ask himself how he is really feeling and what is going on under his premeditated expression (Personal Inventory).

Example:

Let us suppose he is delivering a monologue as part of the scene he is in and he becomes aware that he is planning how to say the next line and how to emotionalize it. At that point he can ask himself what he is really feeling and instead of saying that next line as planned, he would include his real impulses in that moment, allowing the impulses to fill the lines with his real emotional state. Quite often this becomes irreverent to the scene and the author's intentions, but if this technique is used in rehearsal, the irreverence can be acceptable as an exploration. When it is done in a performance, it may be somewhat alien to the character's behavior; but being reconnected with organic reality is much more compelling than premeditated imposition.

I already gave an example of this exercise earlier, but here is a different one:

The actor says the line from a scene: "OK, Mary, war, is that what you want, all-out war?" and at this point he becomes very aware that he has said that line the very same way every time and that he imposes the desired emotion to fill the line with meaning. He stops for a moment, asks himself what he is really feeling, and then includes that as he continues the scene: "So we pull out all the stops and go for blood?" His emotions are different. He is coming from a deeper and more real place, and the line becomes unpredictable to himself and to the other actor. As he continues this process of including his moment-to-moment impulses, his behavior will become more unpredictable and colorful, and if he is using a choice to stimulate the emotional state of the character, the choice will keep him on track, addressing the obligations of the scene.

LEADERSHIP

This is yet another obstacle an actor experiences. It is very close to premeditation and is also attached to his concept of the character's behavior. He has an idea of what the character is feeling and expressing in each moment of the scene, and so he intellectually assumes behavior that he feels should be there, *leading* himself to express the imposed emotions. Unfortunately, none of those expressions come from a real place, so what the actor is really experiencing is pushed down, leaving him with false emotions and behaviors. This is not a rare phenomenon. It is the way most actors function. Over a long period of time they even make their impositional emotions look and feel real. Facilitating emotions and behavior, even when the actor gets good at it, lacks the internal connection with real feelings, which instead become mechanical, uninspiring and predictable. The antidote to leadership is much the same as that for many of the other traps and habits actors fall into. To free yourself you must commit to the exercises and techniques in the pages of this book and must practice them on a daily basis. Almost all of the exercises listed under "Concept" apply to leadership too.

COMMENTARY

This is yet another trap an actor can fall into. It is as if he were standing outside himself while creating a running commentary on what he is doing, or it may manifest itself as a response to any expression that might happen; for example, he might be listening to how he delivers a line and commenting on the level of reality in that delivery. Once he comments, he will short-circuit the flow of his real emotions. It is like derailing a speeding locomotive. At that point he is not connected to his real impulses and must somehow reestablish that connection. Commenting on what the other actor is doing can also create in him a disconnection from what is real.

Commenting is like splitting one's concentration into two separate areas: the involvement with the commentary and the attempted involvement with the choice. When that happens, the actor is functioning inorganically, saying lines and behaving from a cerebral place. So what can he do in order to deal with this short-circuiting commentary? As always, he must first be aware of what is happening. Many actors become so used to working a certain way that they don't even know what is going on, and they forge ahead, delivering lines and assuming behavior over their commentary.

So many of the traps an actor can fall into can be avoided or antidoted with the proper preparation and a solid craft he can turn to. After acknowledging the commentary, the actor must turn that liability into an asset by including it in his expression. If, for example, he is involved in a process that is addressing his obligations and he is relating honestly to the other actor but begins to comment on what he is doing, he can include the emotional impulses that come from that commentary and make them a part of the behavior and the expression of what he is feeling in that moment. By doing that, he avoids the split, and his emotional life and relation to the other actor include the expression of his commentary. Most actors rigidly stick to what they feel should be there and refuse to include in their behavior every impulse that takes place. In real life we feel many things while relating to other people. We have interrupting thoughts and impulses, we get distracted, we comment on how we are affected in the moment, and we usually include all of that commentary as a natural behavior. Unfortunately, when we act, we parenthesize that commentary, creating a split in our concentration and involvement with the responsibilities of the scene. Unless a comment is totally antithetical to the obligations of the material, it should always be included in the actor's expression.

There is an interesting story that I related in *The Diary of a Professional Experiencer* that underscores this issue of commentary. To read about it go to page 300 of that book. That incident opened up a revolutionary concept, at least for me in my work: I believe that if, as a result of his or her commentary, an actor includes the expression of that commentary, in almost all cases the inclusion is acceptable behavior for the character in that circumstance. By including it the actor is functioning on an experiential level.

In addition, it is important to note here that the actor must have a craft, a process to go to that is not only involving but also addresses the obligations of the material and the author's intentions.

TELEGRAPHING

This happens when the actor sends a signal in her behavior, either to the other actor or to the audience, that she is about to express something. It is total premeditation and can be spotted moments before the actual emotional expression. Again, this is the manifestation of being in her head and premeditating behavior. Quite often the actor isn't even aware that she is doing it. For example, she is listening to the other actor who is about to say something funny, and instead of allowing herself to listen and be affected by his statement, she starts to laugh before the other actor has even said the line, telegraphing her response in advance of the impetus to react. In other cases she might knowingly act and express emotional life to let the audience know that she is aware of what is coming.

Telegraphing, just like so many of the other nonorganic habits an actor develops, is a result of not being emotionally involved or affected by the moment-to-moment stimuli one should respond to naturally.

NATURALIZING

This is a very common habit actors fall into. It is what I have called "the limp-wristed school of acting," because these naturalizing actors impose a relaxed state, replete with limp wrists hanging from their arms. They usually lean against something in that feigned relaxed state, move with a "natural" ease, and speak very naturally. It is certainly an attempt to accomplish reality in their acting, but it is actually an assumed state of ease and relaxation worn like an overcoat over what is really happening underneath. Like most of the other traps and habits an actor falls into or develops, it is a totally false state of being, where the actor must impose the emotional life over the actual truth. Many actors succeed in fooling directors and even audiences into believing that they are very natural actors, but the harsh reality is that their work is hollow and lacks connection with their real feelings. It is much like an empty paper bag. The antidote for this phenomenon is much the same as what I have already detailed above. The first step for any actor who falls into this habit is to become conscious of what he is doing and to antidote it by finding out what he is really feeling and expressing that.

CARICATURE

This happens when the actor has an undeveloped idea of what the character is like. He hasn't the knowledge or training to know how to analyze or interpret the components of a character, so he manufactures behaviors and physical gestures that he then assumes as the character. It manifests itself much as a one-dimensional cardboard cutout. It is like wearing an overcoat that has the name of the character pinned to the lapel.

A trained craftsman will read the material, look for what the author says about the character, what the other characters say about him, what he says about himself, and what his behaviors and actions say about him. Once the actor does that, he can create a blueprint of the character, separating the elements into four categories: What is the character like physically? What is he like intellectually? What is he like emotionally? And what is he like psychologically? After the actor has identified and determined the answers to all of those questions, he can ask himself where the similarities are between him and the character. If there are many similarities, he would not have to work to address the differences; however, when there are distinct differences, he would need to work for choices that create them. All of those techniques are specifically detailed in *Irreverent Acting*.

As an acting teacher, I have encountered every problem, block, inhibition, and dependency listed on these pages and quite often have been successful in weaning actors away from those issues. The first step is to make them conscious of what they are doing and of what their habits are. I can then lead them into an organic experience where they are aware of their real impulses and emotions and are able to carry them into the lines. When this occurs, it is an incredible breakthrough for them. They experience the difference between presentation and the real emotion, and there is no denying how that feels. So many of these habits and traps are linked to the deep-seated instrumental issues I discussed earlier, which quite often need to be addressed first.

CREATING A BEING STATE

As an antidote to all of the facilitations, habits and traps he falls into, the actor must first create a being state. A being state is when he can stand or sit and be comfortable, without tension or other blocks, doing no more or less than he feels. It is like starting with an empty blackboard he can write anything on. The actor is not empty; he is **still and full.** Once he has achieved this state of being, he is ready to act. Anything he introduces to himself will affect and change the being state. If, for example, he identifies an obligation related to the material that he is addressing, all he has to do is create a choice—an object, a person, a place, a sound, an odor, or anything else that will affect his being state and stimulate the desired emotional response. Once he has done that, he is experiencing a different being state. So in effect acting is the process of starting with a being state and, by introducing a variety of stimuli, going from one being state to another, virtually fulfilling all of the various obligations of the material. Accomplishing a being state is dependent on a variety of issues. In the first place, the actor has to be conscious of his inhibitions, blocks, dependencies, performance habits that are not organic, and so on. Many of the exercises listed in the early part of this book address the instrumental issues that he needs to eliminate.

THE BEING EXERCISE

This exercise is usually done in front of a group of people or an acting class. I use it quite frequently with my students. The actor is sitting comfortably, facing the class with his legs planted solidly on the floor. His arms and hands may be sitting in his lap. His legs should not be crossed, and his arms should not be folded across his chest. He starts the exercise with Personal Inventory and allows for a stream of consciousness. It is important that he acknowledge all of the "demons": tension, fear, discomfort, or emotional issues that come up while he is doing the exercise. If he exposes all of the things that keep him from a being state, he will ultimately alleviate the ones that stand in the way.

Example (working to achieve a being state):

"How do I feel? I'm tense. I feel on the spot and that there is a great deal expected of me. How do I feel? My palms are sweating. I feel looked at, judged. How do I feel? I feel silly doing this, like a retard! How do I feel? I feel pressure in my chest. My heart is beating really fast. How do I feel? I am avoiding eye contact with the people in the audience. I'm uncomfortable looking at them. How do I feel? Like I want to stop doing this. I feel foolish, like a lab rat being examined. How do I feel? I'm feeling a little vulnerable, and I don't know why. I don't feel comfortable exposing my vulnerability. How do I feel? I'm feeling a little less tense. My heartbeat has slowed down a little. I feel angry, I don't know why. How do I feel? I feel like expressing my anger. I'm angry at all of you out there looking at me and having opinions about me. How do I feel? I feel better having expressed that. How do I feel? I feel like I'm more in touch with what I feel. I feel my body settling into the chair, and I feel more comfortable in my skin. I'm sitting here, and all of a sudden I feel that the people in the audience are on the spot and that I am looking at them and seeing their discomfort. How do I feel? I wonder if that was some kind of projection and I said that to feel better. I don't know, but I feel that my impulses and what I am feeling are flowing more easily. How do I feel? I feel like I don't have to say anything right now. How do I feel? I'm a little insecure. I feel that I don't really know what the hell I'm doing or why I am doing it. I feel better than when I started doing this. I don't know if I am in a being state. I feel more comfortable, but I still feel obligated to do something. How do I feel? I want to stop doing this and sit still and be quiet. I'm going to try that and see what happens. *(He does sit quietly for a few moments and seems somewhat comfortable making eye contact with the audience.)* How do I feel? I feel better. I think that I'm closer to a being state, even though I still feel that I need to do something."

Usually this exercise takes about fifteen or twenty minutes to do. If the actor is successful in eliminating the tension, the self-consciousness, and all of the other obstacles that stand in the way of accomplishing a being state, he can then move on to addressing the scene obligations. Starting from a being state is a profound preparation for attaining the ability to be an experiential actor.

EXPERIENTIAL ACTING

What does experiential acting mean? Stanislavsky said, "The actor must find a way to experience what the character in the play is experiencing." For one hundred years that statement seemed to fall on deaf ears. It is true that Stanislavsky, who is the father of the modern "Method," which he called his "system," had limited practical approaches for accomplishing that. However, he did innovate a system that was revolutionary for that time. Before his contributions, acting was extremely presentational. Actors were taught that certain physical mannerisms were used to communicate certain feelings. A hand turned palm out and placed on the forehead was an indication of stress or sorrow; both hands on the heart were a sign of passion or of a strong feeling of some kind. Actors were actually trained to do those things without truly feeling anything like what the character was really experiencing.

Stanislavsky's system was brought to America by Lee Strasberg and Stella Adler, except that the two of them had complete and diverse interpretations of what Stanislavsky had shared with them. The Group Theater was formed, and that was the beginning of what we now know as the Method. When the Group Theater disbanded, several splinter groups carried the mantle forward. The Actors Studio was started in New York in 1947, while another group, called the Actors Lab, settled in Hollywood. Over the years and because of the translation of Stanislavsky's books, the method was picked up by scores of teachers around the country. In my opinion, however, their interpretation was questionable. For example, sense memory, one of the important Stanislavsky techniques, is so misunderstood and so badly taught that when actors come to my classes and attempt to use it, I can see that they are totally confused as to how it is done or applied.

So what then is experiential acting and how does an actor achieve it? I have been working with actors for a period of fifty years and have developed what I believe is a complete system of acting. It is divided into two major areas: the instrument and the craft. As I said at the beginning of this book, the instrument must be liberated so that the actor is free to act. That liberation is a process of stripping away all the inhibitions, blocks, obstacles, dependencies, and the damage sustained while living in our society. It involves confronting those obstacles and eliminating them. Craft, on the other hand, is the process of identifying the responsibilities and obligations of material and of finding "choices" that will address and fulfill them. So if we go back to Stanislavsky's original statement, "The actor must...experience what the character...is experiencing," the way that is accomplished is that the actor identifies what the character is experiencing and from his own frame of reference, his own life, uses personal impelling choices to create the parallel reality of the character in the piece.

Let us use a hypothetical example: The character is sitting at a desk with a pistol in his hand, contemplating suicide. He speaks many lines defining his depression and the reasons for wanting to take his life. His lines are filled with remorse, self-hatred and a complete feeling of failure. If the actor playing the part wants to experience all that the character is feeling, he must find those realities in his own life. Many people at low ebb think about ending their lives, but fortunately the depression passes and they go on living. The actor must selectively emphasize his own feelings of failure and desperation, and, if ever he has thought about suicide, he must resurrect the issues that made him contemplate it. He can do this in a variety of ways. Since at this point I am not going to get deeply into an explanation of the craft, I will only say that by using his own parallel realities the actor can create the emotional state the character is in. Becoming a "professional experiencer" is predicated on taking the journey into the process and learning how to stimulate the desired emotional states one is obligated to.

INSTRUMENTAL PREPARATIONS

PREPARING INSTRUMENTALLY FOR A REHEARSAL

When actors approach doing a scene, so many of them just pick up the script and begin to read the lines. They endow the words with assumed emotions and repeat that process until they have learned the lines and have solidified the emotions they have imposed. That is when they decide to show the scene in a class or at an audition. Their real feelings and impulses have been ignored and suppressed, and they are functioning robotically. Preparation is ninety-five percent of being able to act. If you are not prepared, you cannot function from a real place.

So where does an actor start to prepare instrumentally for getting ready to address the material? The first step should always be dealing with tension. There is obvious tension that he is aware of, and there is subliminal tension that he may not be aware of. There is also mental tension, which gets in the way of being able to focus. Earlier in this book I detailed a large number of relaxation exercises designed to free the actor of tension.

EXPANDED PERSONAL INVENTORY

Once the actor has eliminated his tension he should do an Expanded Personal Inventory to see where he is emotionally and to ascertain his ability to become selflessly involved. Expanded Personal Inventory in an instrumental area is done by asking oneself where one is instrumentally in relation to where one needs to be for the beginning of the scene one is about to address.

Example:

I have just completed my relaxation exercises, and I feel that I have eliminated the tension; but where am I emotionally in terms of where I need to be for the beginning of the scene? I do feel relaxed, but the character is very vulnerable in the beginning. So I need to do an interim preparation to elevate my vulnerability, because I don't feel affectable at all!

At that point the actor would select an exercise that would make him more available and vulnerable. He could do an imaginary monologue, talking to someone in his life about the issues between them that might make him vulnerable, or a Coffin Monologue—an exercise I have already explained in the section on the fear of being vulnerable. Another good technique for preparing to rehearse is Observe, Perceive, and Wonder, which I detailed under "Compensational Behavior."

THE TWO-PERSON BEING WORKOUT

This is a wonderful preparation for getting ready to rehearse with another person. It is a three-part exercise. The first part is designed to establish a being state between the actor and his scene partner; the second is a selfless-involvement approach and can be an observation, perception and wonderment involvement; and the third is an ensemble workout.

Example (first part):

The two actors stand or sit facing each other and start by expressing how they feel and acknowledging all of the obstacles and commentary that get in the way of expressing their real feelings in the moment and about each other. It is done in a conversational framework.

He starts: "I feel a little self-conscious, and it's because you are looking at me with some intensity."

She responds, "I feel amused by that. I am not intense, just interested."

He responds, "I feel a little better. I still feel anxious. I feel like I should be doing more than I'm doing."

She responds, "I feel a little obligated also."

He responds, "I'm attracted to you, and that makes me very nervous. I mean I am not coming on to you, but I had to expose that so I could move on and be OK in the moment."

She pauses and then says, "I am flattered, and I understand that it is sometimes difficult to deal with the sexual issue and keep your mind on the work."

He blushes and takes a moment before saying the following: "I feel better now. If this exercise is supposed to establish a being state between us, I guess that we have to be totally honest and expose all of the things that get in the way of that."

She smiles and agrees.

This part can continue until both actors feel comfortable with themselves and with each other. The second part of the exercise, Observe, Perceive, and Wonder, has already been explained.

The actors then do the third part, Ensemble, by working to create an ensemble state between the two of them and hopefully accomplish a creative dependency on each other. I already explained the exercise and gave an example of it in the section on compensational behavior, but here's another:

Example (third part):

They continue relating to each other verbally. He starts: "I like the way you express your feelings."

She responds, "That makes me feel good."

HE: Now I feel like I said the right thing.

SHE: I feel like you are ingratiating now, and that makes me feel like I doubt your sincerity.

HE: Now I feel a little hurt by your response.

SHE: I feel bad because of the way you responded to my impulse.

HE: Now I feel embarrassed.

SHE: I feel sorry that I offended you.

HE: I feel better that you said that.

SHE: You make me feel like I have to be careful about what I say to you.

HE: That makes me feel a little defensive.

SHE: I feel like I don't know how to respond to that.

HE: I feel confused at the moment.

SHE: That makes me feel like I would like to tell you that I like working with you.

HE: Now I feel better, thank you.

SHE: I didn't say it to make you more comfortable. I really mean it.

HE: I feel positive about our relationship.

SHE: That makes me feel good.

Here again, the actors can do each of the three parts of the exercise for as long as it takes to establish an ensemble state between them. Once they feel ready to work with each other, they can start to address the obligations of the scene, using a craft approach. There are ten sample rehearsals detailed in my book *Acting from the Ultimate Consciousness.*

PREPARING INSTRUMENTALLY FOR AN AUDITION

Usually this is a one-person involvement, but it can also be an audition that the actor is preparing to do with another actor. If that is the case, she should do all of the exercises listed above. If she is working to prepare alone, she should address her tension and anxiety, using any of the relaxation exercises. When she feels relaxed, she might check her ego state. If her ego or self-esteem is not as strong as it should be, she can do a variety of ego preparations, such as counting her blessings and accomplishments (already explained). She may need to stimulate a positive state of being by doing a Pollyanna workout (also explained in the section on self-esteem). In addition, she should also do some selfless involvement to get out of herself. That can be accomplished when she is in the waiting room before going into the audition. She just gets selflessly involved in the environment and with all the people there. Of course, the audition is dependent on addressing the obligations of the material, which requires knowledge of craft; but here we are only dealing with the instrumental responsibilities; the craft process is another issue.

INSTRUMENTAL PREPARATION TO PERFORM

Everything listed above should be done when preparing for a performance.

CRAFT IGNORANCE

Over the many years I have been teaching I have had actors come to me from a multitude of acting teachers in Hollywood, New York, and Europe. Those actors come for me to help them prepare for an audition, or they join one of my classes. Almost all of them do a monologue, a scene, or an audition piece. When they are finished, I ask them *how* they approached what they just did. In almost ninety-eight percent of the cases they have no specific process or knowledge of what they are doing or how they did what I just saw. I get these kinds of answers to my question: I put myself in the character's place; I imagined that this was happening to me; I thought about his feelings and I used them; I remembered having felt that way; I used the given circumstances; I pretended that it was happening to me; I saw what I was supposed to be feeling in my inner self. There are many other such explanations for how they delivered the scene or monologue, none of which is a process of creating organic reality or an impetus to behave. All of their explanations are cerebral, starting in the head and remaining there, only allowing them to assume behaviors that they are not experiencing in reality. It is tragic that in the thirty-two or thirty-three hundred years since the first actor, acting has not kept up with man's technical advance and evolution. The training of actors has lagged decades behind advances in psychology, science, technology and almost every other field.

What motivated and drove me to create a specific craft process was the frustration I experienced as a young actor not being able to find the *how*. When I would ask a teacher or coach, "How do you do that?" he or she would supply vague intellectual answers that fell far short of explaining how something was achieved. It took me a while to come to the conclusion that the reason they could not answer my question was that they didn't know how. A perfect example of an acting teacher who enjoyed quite a reputation was Alvina Krause, my teacher at Northwestern University. The two years I attended her classes were the most frustrating of my life. Whenever I would ask her how to approach a scene, she would get impatient with me and give me vague answers, which made me look stupid. Eventually I stopped asking her. It was very disappointing to learn that some of my other teachers had also developed a reputation of being important in the field, and extremely frustrating that I was still without specific answers as to how to create the realities I was obligated to. When I finally found a teacher who had some answers and could deal with the question of how, it was like discovering an oasis in the desert. He certainly didn't have all the answers—I'm sure nobody does—but for the first time on my learning journey I had a few letters of the alphabet, so to speak, which allowed me to spell words. I had the beginning of a process. Over the many years that followed I created, discovered, and innovated a complete craft, which gets a little more complete every year. In my book *Irreverent Acting,* which is totally dedicated to the craft and system that I teach, you can learn all the parts of the approach, as well as the specific techniques designed to address dramatic material and fulfill it.

AN ADDITIONAL WORD ABOUT CRAFT

Putting it into a less technical frame, it all boils down to the three parts of craft: **obligation, choice,** and **choice approach.** The actor asks himself, *What is it that I want to experience, to feel? What can I use from my own life to stimulate that experience? And how can I create the what that will impel me to feel what I need to feel?* The last question relates to the choice approach, which is how you create the choice. At present I have thirty-one choice ap-proaches, listed and detailed in my six other books.

IN CONCLUSION

All of the instrumental obstacles I have written about in this book, the fears, the insecurities, the dependencies, and all of the other issues that instrumentally block an actor—as well as all of the facilitations, habits and traps he develops and falls into—have been explored. I outlined and described a great number of exercises and techniques to eliminate those problems and suggested how the actor must come from a truly organic place in order to be real. Those issues do not go away. In time they grow older and more solidly entrenched as the actor ages. Unless he can antidote and eliminate them, he will never be able to become an organic **experiential actor.**

I have worked with thousands of actors all over the world, and I know from experience that if a person does the work, follows the blueprint and the exercise structures, not only will he/she eliminate the obstacles and problems, but he/she will become a much more organic actor and realize the fulfillment of experiencing the reality of the character he/she is playing. That is what makes a great actor!

INDEX OF EXERCISES
AND TECHNIQUES